T0065298

Pen of a Ready Writer

TRACY NEAL

WESTBOW
PRESS®
A DIVISION OF THOMAS NELSON
& ZONDERVAN

WestBow Press books may be ordered through booksellers or by contacting:

WestBow Press
A Division of Thomas Nelson & Zondervan
1663 Liberty Drive
Bloomington, IN 47403
www.westbowpress.com
1 (866) 928-1240

ISBN: 978-1-5127-0590-4 (sc)
ISBN: 978-1-5127-0591-1 (e)

Library of Congress Control Number: 2015912249

Print information available on the last page.

WestBow Press rev. date: 10/15/2015

Contents

Complaining Won't Make it Better 1

Happy Birthday Mom 3

Set Free 5

Words Cant Explain The Pain 7

In the Mist of it All 8

I Appreciate You Tam! 10

The Master 12

Wait 14

Peace on Earth 16

What Goes Around Come Around 17

Cheating Man 19

Blessing from A-Z 21

My Life was Spared 23

God Don't Put More on You.... Then You Can't Bear! 25

Friends Today Enemies Tomorrow 27

Same Script Different Cast 29

As the Days Go By 31

Why Do We 33

Jesus Spared They Life 35

Never Question God 37

Independent Women 39

Something I Have to Say 41

You Know You are a Child of God When…........................... 43

Death Clock.. 45

Pray.. 47

Dead Beat Dads 48

Congratulation 50

I Am Me.. 52

Still Broken 53

Always on Time...55

Who Cares 56

Wait There's More.. 58

To My Beautiful Sister 60

Take Care... and Careless... 61

Peeked Into My Future 63

Happy Mother's Day.. 65

Life.. 66

Let Your Mess... Be Your Message.................... 67

Just the 2 of Us 69

Get Insured by Chirst...................................... 71

Get Tested/Be Protected 73

Follow Me…...75

Don't Steal 77

Don't Leave Your Family Broken 79

Call on the Lord... 81

Know Your Worth 82

Beautiful Sister Nek 84

Count Your Blessings 86

Thank You for Loving Me................................ 88

Who Am I…? 90

About the Author 95

About the Book.. 97

Complaining Won't Make it Better

EVERYDAY, WE ALL HAVE TO DEAL WITH SOMETHING IN OUR LIFE…SOME TYPE OF HEADACHE OR HEARTACHE, ITS ALWAYS ONE THING AFTER ANOTHER… BUT WHY WORRY, WHY PULL YOUR HAIR OUT, WHY COMPLAIN, IS ANY OF THESE THINGS WE DO GONE MAKE IT BETTER? "NO" OF COURSE NOT…. SO WHAT WE ALL NEED TO DO IS START FOCUSING ON THE LORD, TRUST, PRAY, BELIEVE AND HAVE FAITH. AND GOD WILL SEE YOU THROUGH… HE DID IT FOR ME, AND I KNOW HE WILL DO IT FOR YOU… THE LORD SAID DO YOUR BEST, AND HE WILL DO THE REST… WE HAVE TO REALIZE WE HAVE MORE TO BE THANKFUL FOR THEN TO WORRY ABOUT…. WE MUST GO THROUGH THE STORM TO APPRECIATE THE SUNSHINE….. WHEN WE COMPLAIN, WE REMAIN, BUT WHEN WE PRAISE WE RAISE….

LIFE IT SELF IS A STRUGGLE, WE CAN HANDLE IT, BECAUSE GOD DON'T PUT MORE ON YOU THEN U CAN BEAR.... WHEN YOU SIT UP AND COMPLAIN YOU JUST OPENING THE DOOR MORE AND MORE FOR THE DEVIL, LIKE YOU INVITING HIM IN. DON'T LEAVE ROOM FOR COMPLAINING, FILL YOUR HEART WITH THANKFULNESS, THE DEVIL CANT GET IN WHEN YOU ARE THANKFUL, TRY THANKING GOD, IN GOOD TIMES AND IN BAD, FROM NOW ON LOOK AT THAT BILL, PROBLEM, WORRY, HURT, PAIN, ENEMY, AND THAT THING YOU NEED TO BE DELIVERED FROM IN THE FACE AND SAY, YOU A BIG THING TO ME, BUT A SMALL THING TO MY GOD, AND I CAN AND WILL OVERCOME ANYTHING BECAUSE ANYTHING IS POSSIBLE TO THOSE WHO BELIEVE, REMEMBER KEEP YOUR MIND ON HEAVEN, BECAUSE GOD HAVE MORE TO OFFER US THEN THIS WORLD, WE CAN HAVE PEACE REAL JOY, HAPPINESS, NO PAIN, NO MORE TEARS, NO SUFFERING, NO DEATH, NO BILLS, NO KILLING, NO WORRY, NO HEADACHE, NO HEARTACHE, SO IF YOU WANT TO GO TO THAT PREFECT PLACE... ASK GOD RIGHT NOW TO SET YOU FREE, BECAUSE WHO THE SON SET FREE IS FREE INDEED...

Happy Birthday Mom

WE WILL LIKE TO SAY HAPPY BIRTHDAY TO A
WONDERFUL PERSON,WE WILL MAKE A BIG FUSS…..
ITS BLACK CHERRY WE MUST…..BECAUSE IF IT WASN'T
FOR HER,THERE WILL BE NO US, SHE HAD FOUR
BEAUTIFUL GIRLS, WHO LOVE HER AND MISS HER
SO! IT WILL NEVER BE O.K.WE WILL NEVER LET HER
GO…WORDS CANT EXPLAIN THE PAIN, AND LIFE
FOR US WILL NEVER BE THE SAME…SHE WAS THE
NUMBER 1 QUEEN…WHO MADE IT TO THE TOP…SHE
LOVE TO SING,DANCE,TELL GHOST STORIES,AND
SHE WAS A FIGHTER SHE COULDN'T BE STOPPED!
SHE HAD LIFE HERE! BUT SHE FREE THERE! THE
MOTHER DAUGHTER RELATIONSHIP WE ALL HAD
NO ONE CAN EVER COMPARE! AND FOR ALL HER
FAMILY MEMBERS SHE WAS THERE… I CANT STRESS
HOW MUCH WE LOVE AND MISS HER! BUT IN THE
WORDS OF CARLA [KEEP IT SIMPLE] SO LET ME END
THIS WITH A SMILE SHE ALWAYS TOLD ME OF US, SHE

WAS VERY PROUD,WE NEVER CHANGED,WE DIDN'T CARE IF SHE WAS RIGHT OR WRONG WE TREATED HER THE SAME..WITH LOVE AND RESPECT...AND THAT PUT A SMILE ON HER FACE THAT HER GIRLS GOT HER BACK! [CARLA] YOU ARE A WONDERFUL MOTHER,GRAND MOTHER,AUNT,SISTER,AND FRIEND WE LOVE YOU THUR THICK AND THIN….. AND WE ALL ARE HERE TO SAY...WE LOVE YOU AND MISS YOU….AND HAPPY BIRTHDAY!

Set Free

EACH DAY WE THOUGHT YOU WERE COMING
HOME, BUT ALL ALONG YOU WAS GOING HOME.
GOD PREPARED US IN EVERY WAY AND GAVE US
STRENGTH FOR THIS VERY DAY, AND I AM PROUD TO
SAY "MOM" YOU CAME A VERY LONG WAY. YOU KEPT
US HAPPY, YOU MADE US SMILE, YOU GO GIRL, YOU
MADE US PROUD......YOU'VE BEEN THROUGH A LOT,
SOME DAYS IT WAS ROUGH, BUT GOD SAID, ENOUGH
IS ENOUGH, YOUR WORK HERE IS DONE.....AND I CAN
UNDERSTAND WHY YOU WHERE THE CHOSEN ONE
BECAUSE YOU HAD A HEART OF GOLD. YOU WERE A
GIVER, VERY SWEET, AND IT WAS TIME FOR YOU AND
JESUS TO MEET. YOU ARE IN HEAVEN NOW WHERE
YOU WILL ALWAYS BE FINE, AND RIGHT ABOUT NOW
THIS SHOULD BE A HAPPY TIME. ITS NOT ABOUT
WHAT YOU HAVE OR WHAT YOU DON'T HAVE, IT'S
WHO YOU HAVE, "JESUS" IS WHO WE HAVE AND WHO
WE NEED.'GOD' PICKED "MOM" OUT FROM ALL THE

REST, DON'T QUESTION HIM CAUSE GOD KNOWS WHATS BEST. "BLACK CHERRY" YOU ALWAYS WANTED YOUR OWN PLACE, BUT YOU'RE IN A MANISON NOW AND YOU GOT NOTHING BUT SPACE. I WISH I COULD TAKE YOUR PLACE, YOU GET TO MEET JESUS FACE TO FACE, NO MORE SUFFERING, NO MORE GRIEF FROM ALL THAT PAIN.YOU'VE BEEN RELEASED AND NOW YOU HAVE PEACE, AND I UNDERSTAND THAT YOU ARE WITH THE "MASTER" NOW.... YOU'RE IN GODS HAND! THE THING THAT KEEP ME STRONG IS THAT I KNOW THIS IS NOT THE END, WE WILL REUNITE WITH "CARLA" AGAIN. WE WILL NEVER PART BECAUSE WHEN YOU LEFT YOU TOOK HALF OF MY HEART......BUT WE'VE GOT TO HOLD ON AND BE STRONG AND LIVE ON BECAUSE OUR HEAVENLY FATHER WON'T STEER US WRONG! LOVE YOU "BLACK CHERRY " YOU MEAN THE WORLD TO ME AND THANK YOU "LORD" FOR SETTING "MOM " FREE!

Words Cant Explain The Pain

PAIN ON THE OUTSIDE….. PAIN WITHIN……WHERE SHOULD I START? WHERE DO I BEGIN? WHEN U LOSE SOMEONE….. YOUR MOTHER ……. WHAT DO YOU DO………….? PLEASE DON'T SPEAK UNLESS IT HAPPENED TO YOU! YOU CAN'T TELL ME HOW TO FEEL, IM SO ANGRY AND BITTER INSIDE, I WISH I COULD HUG HER….. TURN BACK THE HANDS OF TIME….I CAN'T EXPLAIN HOW I FEEL… IT'S A VOID ITS UNREAL, IT'S NOT RIGHT, IT'S NOT FAIR…SOMEBODY PLEASE WAKE ME UP FROM THIS NIGHTMARE!!!!! HOW CAN THIS HAPPEN, WILL THE HURT AND PAIN EVER LEAVE……I WILL NEVER GET OVER IT!! IT'S STILL SO HARD TO BELIEVE!! I WILL HAVE MY MOMENTS EVERYDAY FOR THE REST OF MY LIFE. I WILL PRAY, I WILL CRY, AND I WILL ALWAYS WONDER WHY? HOW COULD THIS HAPPEN? HOW COULD THIS BE? HOW COULD THIS HAPPEN TO MY FAMILY? IT'S HURTFUL… IT'S HARD…. IT'S SAD…. I AM ANGRY BITTER AND MAD!!!!! IT HURT, AND IT'S A DRAIN ITS HARD TO WRITE…BECAUSE WORDS CANT EXPLAIN THE PAIN!

In the Mist of it All

I KNOW THAT HE WILL COME THROUGH…. BECAUSE HE ALWAYS DO, SO DON'T GIVE UP, DON'T LOOSE FAITH, HE'S NEVER TO EARLY, HE'S NEVER TO LATE, SO ALL YOU HAVE TO DO IS PRAY AND WAIT. THE LORD DON'T PUT MORE ON YOU THEN YOU CANT BEAR…. SO STAND STRONG, BECAUSE JESUS IS STANDING RIGHT THERE. DON'T LET NO MAN ON EARTH GET YOU DOWN… DON'T LET THE DEVIL SEE YOU FROWN…. IF YOU HAVE WORRIES OR PROBLEMS….. DON'T HOLD ON TO IT, DON'T LET IT SHOW, THINK OF ALL JESUS DID FOR YOU AND LET IT GO!!!!! YOU MIGHT FEEL UNLOVED, UNWANTED, ALONE AND CONFUSED, BUT DON'T GIVE UP…….. OPEN THE DOOR BECAUSE GOD WANNA USE YOU… OPEN UP YOUR HEART, OPEN UP YOUR MIND, YOU WAISTED ENOUGH TIME, SHAKE OFF THE DISAPPOINTMENT, FAILURE, THE HURT AND THE PAIN. THANK HIM FOR ALL YOU BEEN THROUGH BECAUSE AFTER ALL THAT PAIN YOU HAVE PLENTY

OF BLESSINGS TO GAIN…THE LORD IS STILL CALLING YOUR NAME... HE LOVE YOU MORE THEN WORDS CAN SAY... YOU MIGHT BE ON THE ROAD…… BUT YOU'RE GOING THE WRONG WAY….. SO STOP AND PRAY. BEFORE YOU GET TO FAR GONE… AND HEAD IN THE RIGHT DIRECTION AND LET GOD LEAD YOU ON…. IF EVERYTHING SEEM LIKE IT'S NOT GOING YOUR WAY…. OR NOT GOING RIGHT, THAT'S THE LIFE YOU CHOOSE….. YOU DIDN'T GIVE UP A FIGHT…. IF YOU ARE DEPRESSED, STRESSED, AND YOU JUST WANNA BE FREE, THINK OF LIFE AS A PUZZLE… "JESUS" IS THE MISSING PIECE!!! PUT THAT PIECE TO YOUR PUZZLE, AND MAKE YOUR LIFE COMPLETE. SOME PEOPLE STAND STRONG, SOME FALL, BUT JESUS IS THERE, HE CARE, AND HE LOVE US….. IN THE MIST OF IT ALL!!

I Appreciate You Tam!

I APPRECIATE YOU AND THE THINGS THAT YOU DID,
YOU ARE A STRONG BLACK WOMAN WHO HOLDS
IT DOWN, AND THAT I DIG...... I APPRECIATE THE
FACT YOU ALWAYS GOT MY BACK, I CAN TELL YOU
A SECRET AND IT WILL NEVER GET BACK, TO YOU I
CAN TALK, I CAN LAUGH, I CAN CRY, YOU MY RIGHT
HAND GIRL WHEN I CRY YOU CRY..... YOU MY LEGS
WHEN I CAN T STAND, MY VOICE WHEN I CAN'T
TALK, EARS TO LISTEN, HAND TO HOLD, AND
TOGETHER WE CAN WALK.... YOU MY SHOULDER
TO CRY ON, DEPEND ON, RELIE ON, YOU TAM LOVE
MY SISTER ALWAYS MY BACK BONE... YOU MY GIRL,
MY WORLD, AND YOU NEVER LET ME DOWN, YOU
GOT MY BACK, I GOT YOUR BACK WITH US THAT'S
HOW IT GO DOWN.... I CAN CALL YOU RIGHT NOW
AND YOU ALWAYS COME THROUGH.... I DON'T CARE
WHAT IT IS I WILL GIVE MY LAST TO YOU, CANT SAY
NOTHING BAD ABOUT YOU, YOU AN INDEPENDENT

WOMAN THAT'S WHY WE SMILE AT YOU… YOU HAVE A HEART OF GOLD, YOU ARE AS GOOD AS IT GETS…. WHEN GOD WAS PICKING SISTERS… MAN IM GLAD I WAS PICKED…. MY FRIEND, MY SISTER, MY GIRL, MY LIFE…. I GOT YOUR BACK UNTIL THE END IF YOU'RE WRONG OR IF YOU'RE RIGHT…. YOU GOT IT GOING ON, NO MATTER WHAT NOBODY SAY, THIS TO YOU MY GIRL, HAPPY BIRTHDAY AND APPRECIATION DAY!

The Master

NO MATTER WHAT YOU ARE GOING THROUGH, GOD IS ALWAYS THERE FOR YOU. TIMES SEEMS HARD BUT IT WILL GET BETTER, THINGS SEEM WRONG, BUT YOU GO THROUGH THINGS TO GET STRONG. PEOPLE MAKE MISTAKES, WE ALL DO, BUT JESUS WILL SEE US THROUGH, WHO CARES WHAT PEOPLE THINK, HOW THEY FEEL, OR WHAT THEY SAY, IT'S UP JESUS IF IM GONE BE HERE ANOTHER DAY. SO THEY CAN TALK, THEY CAN LAUGH, AND IN THE END THEY WILL SEE, ONLY GOD NOT PEOPLE CAN JUDGE ME…. HE'S THE HEAD OF OUR LIFE, WHEN THINGS GO WRONG, HE WILL MAKE IT RIGHT…… HE IS OUR PROVIDER, OUR PROTECTION, AND OUR SAVIOR. HE IS WILLING AND HE IS ABLE, SO DON'T LET THINGS IN LIFE GET YOU UPSET, BECAUSE GOD IS'NT FINISH WITH YOU YET…… I KNOW IT'S HARD, WHEN IT RAINS IT POURS…. BUT WHILE IT'S RAINING, PRAY MORE AND MORE….. DON'T GIVE UP BECAUSE GOD

HAS SOMETHING GOOD IN STORE…. SO BEFORE I GO I HAVE A FEW MORE THINGS TO SAY… JESUS IS HIS NAME…. IT MIGHT BE HARD, BUT NO DAY IS THE SAME…. HE SEE YOUR PAIN, YOUR TEARS, HE HEARS YOU WHEN YOU CALL… BECAUSE HE RIGHT THERE IN THE MIST OF IT ALL… IT'S GONE GET BETTER, THIS IS SOMETHING YOU CANT FIX….. JUST HOLD ON DON'T QUIT, AND LET THE MAN IN CHARGE HANLDE THIS!

Wait

WAIT, WAIT, WAIT, EVERYBODY HAVE TO WAIT...

YOU HAVE TO WAIT ON EVERYTHING,

YOU HAVE TO WAIT AT THE CLINIC,

YOU HAVE TO WAIT AT THE DENTIST, WAIT ON A
BUS.... EVEN IF YOU ARE IN A RUSH,

YOU HAVE TO WAIT 9 MONTHS WHILE YOU CARRY
YOUR CHILD

YOU HAVE TO WAIT UNTIL THEY GROW UP AND IT'S
GONE BE A WHILE,

YOU HAVE TO WAIT ON YOUR PAY CHECK AFTER A
LONG 2WEEKS OF WORK,

YOU HAVE TO WAIT ON YOUR MATE, YOU HAVE TO
WAIT TO YOU ARE OLDER ENOUGH TO DATE,

YOU HAVE TO WAIT IN THE HOSPITAL, WHEN YOU ARE
IN PAIN

YOU HAVE TO WAIT TO SEE WHO GONE WIN AT THE
END OF A GAME

YOU HAVE WAIT TO BE RELEASED WHEN YOU ARE IN
JAIL,

YOU HAVE TO WAIT ON YOUR TEST RESULTS IF YOU
PASS OR IF YOU FAIL

YOU HAVE TO WAIT ON YOUR BIRTHDAY WHICH IS
ONCE A YEAR,

YOU HAVE TO WAIT ON YOUR FOOD UNTIL ITS DONE,

YOU HAVE TO WAIT UNTIL DAY BREAK COME,

YOU HAVE TO WAIT ON DEATH IF IT'S FAR OR NEAR

WAITING IS A PART OF LIFE… THINGS COME WHEN
IT COME… BUT DON'T WAIT TO GET RIGHT AND
TIME WAITS FOR NO ONE…..

Peace on Earth

PEACE ON EARTH IS A BEAUTIFUL THING, PEOPLE NEED TO COME TOGETHER IN THE TIME OF NEED, LOVE ONE ANOTHER, AND PRAY FOR EACH OTHER, AND HAPPY YOU WILL BE. TREAT PEOPLE THE WAY YOU WANT TO BE TREATED… AND YOU WILL BE SET FREE. RESPECT, SHARING, CARING, AND GIVE FROM YOUR HEART…. BE A PEACE MAKER, NOT A HEART BREAKER, WALK AWAY BEFORE IT START... LOVE IS THE ANSWER, LOVE IS THE KEY… LOVE NOT ONLY YOUR LOVE ONES, BUT ALSO YOUR ENEMY... REMEMBER LOVE COVERS A MULTITUDE OF SINS, JUST KEEP ON GIVING LOVE AND SHOWING LOVE UNTIL THE END… EVERYONE NEED PEACE ALL THE TIME, ANY PLACE, IT SHOULD NEVER BE ABOUT RACE… IF YOU ARE TIRED OF THE WARS, HATE, KILLING, PAIN, AND HURT, START WITH YOU, DO YOUR PART SO WE CAN HAVE PEACE ON EARTH!

What Goes Around Come Around

WHAT GOES AROUND COMES AROUND, OH YEA IT'S
TRUE, WHATEVER YOU DO TO SOMEONE IT'S COMING
RIGHT BACK TO YOU, SO DON'T THINK YOU ARE
GETTING AWAY WITH DOING SOMEONE WRONG, ALL
THINGS MUST COME TO AN END, TREATING PEOPLE
WRONG WONT LAST FOR LONG. TREAT PEOPLE THE
WAY YOU WANT TO BE TREATED... IF YOU CAN'T
RESPECT A PERSON, LEAVE THEM... WHY HOLD ON
TO DO THEM WRONG... IF A PERSON CAN GET YOU
THAT UPSET MOVE ON... HOW IN THE WORLD DO
YOU WANNA BE IN CONTROL, WHEN YOU CAN'T
CONTROL YOURSELF...? GET A LIFE, GET SOME HELP,
IF YOU THINK YOU NOT DOING A PERSON WRONG,
THEN YOU REALLY HAVE A PROBLEM, GET SOME
HELP, PRAY ABOUT IT, SOLVE IT. HURTING A PERSON
FEELINGS THAT'S NOT COOL, PUTTING A PERSON

DOWN SO U CAN FEEL LIKE YOU UP… YOU MUST BE A FOOL… AND THE PERSON THAT SAID STICKS AND STONES MAY BREAK MY BONES BUT WORDS WILL NEVER HURT ME… THAT'S A LIE… BECAUSE WORDS HURT MORE THEN ANYTHING… YOU WANT ME TO TELL YOU WHY… IF YOU GET HIT WITH A STICK IT HURT FOR A FEW, BUT WORDS WILL DEFINITELY STICK WITH YOU… WORDS DO HURT, BUT YOU MUST KNOW YOU'RE WORTH… AND KNOW WHO YOU ARE… WHATEVER THEY CALLING YOU THEY MORE CLOSE TO IT, THAT'S NOT WHO YOU ARE BY FAR … THE PERSON THAT'S DOING WRONG GONE GET WHATS COMING… THEY NOT GONE BE HAPPY THEY GONE BE RUNNING... JUST WATCH IF YOU KEEP ON DOING PEOPLE WRONG, AND PUTTING THEM DOWN, JUST KNOW WHAT GOES AROUND, COMES BACK AROUND

Cheating Man

FIRST OF ALL LET ME START OFF BY SAYING, DON'T NO GOOD WOMAN NEED A CHEATING MAN, MEN WANNA HAVE THEY CAKE AND EAT IT TO... THEY WANNA DO WHAT THEY WANNA DO.... A MAN WANNA BE WITH A WOMAN THAT'S REAL AND TRUE, BUT STILL WANNA CHEAT ON YOU... I DON'T SEE WHY MEN WANNA CHEAT... I GUESS BECAUSE THEY ARE TOO BLIND TO SEE. THEY DON'T KNOW HOW TO ACT, BECAUSE THEY NEVER HAD A REAL WOMAN LIKE THAT. THEY WANNA GIVE THEM PROBLEMS, I DON'T UNDERSTAND... THEY HAVE A GOOD WOMAN RIGHT THERE BUT THEY'RE OUT THERE PLAYING... EVERY GOOD WOMAN NEED A GOOD MAN, MEN SHOULDN'T CHEAT BECAUSE CHEATERS NEVER WIN, SOME MEN CHEAT TO PROVE A POINT TO THEIR FRIENDS... BUT WHAT GO AROUND COME AROUND, YOU WILL SEE IN THE END... MEN CHEAT AND HOLD ON TO A GOOD WOMAN, DON'T TRY TO BRING A GOOD WOMAN DOWN, SHE BETTER

OFF WITHOUT YOU AROUND... WHY DO MEN WANNA
BE WITH THIS AND THAT? WHEN THAT MAN SHOULD
BE FAITHFUL AND GIVE HIS WOMAN THE UTMOST
RESPECT BECAUSE IF THE SHOE WAS ON THE OTHER
FOOT, A MAN CAN'T TAKE IT I BET... ONE DAY THAT
WOMAN GONE GET FED UP, SHE GONE BE TIRED OF
YOU AND ALL YOU DO... SHE NOT GONE KEEP ON
BEING A FOOL, SHE GONE TELL YOU IT'S NOT UP TO
YOU NO MORE AND SHE GONE CHOSE... AND THAT'S
THE DAY SHE GONE WALK AWAY, YOU GONE KNOW
IT AND YOU WILL SEE, YOU CAN HAVE ALL THE
WOMAN YOU WANT, BUT NOT HOLDING ON TO ME...
A MAN SHE WILL FIND... A REAL WOMAN YOU WILL
REALLY HAVE TO SEEK... BUT YOU WILL NEVER FIND
ONE BECAUSE YOU CANT BE FAITHFUL YOU LOVE TO
CHEAT

Blessing from A-Z

A ROOF OVER MY HEAD

BILLS GOT PAID WHEN I WAS ON EDGE

CHILD HAS HER HEALTH AND STRENGTH

DID THINGS I DIDN'T DESERVE

EVERYTHING ABOUT ME NOT

RIGHT, I GOT MY NERVES

FORGIVE ME FOR ALL MY SINS, AND

FORGET BECAUSE HE CAN

GAVE ME LIFE BECAUSE, FOR ME HE HAS PLANS

HAVE EVERYTHING, I WANT AND NEED

I'M TO BLESSED TO BE STRESSED OR DEPRESSED,

THAT'S WHY IM HAPPY AND FREE

JOB TO GO TO EVERYDAY

KEEP ME HEALTHY..... WITH TRANSPORTATION,

SO AT MY JOB I CAN STAY

LOVE ME WITH ALL HIS HEART

MAKE ME HAPPY, EVEN WHEN I DON'T DO MY PART

NEVER LET ME DOWN

OPEN EARS FOR ME WHEN NO ONE'S AROUND

PROTECT ME, FAMILY AND MY FRIENDS TOO

QUIT, HE WILL NEVER BECAUSE HE'S TRUE

RUN TO HIM WITH OPEN ARMS FOR ME AND FOR YOU

STRONG MIND, HEALTH AND STRENGTH

AND THINGS FOR ME TO SHARE

TRUST ME TO HANDLE THINGS, HE DON'T PUT

NOTHING ON YOU THEN YOU CANT BEAR

UTMOST RESPECT TO MY WONDERFUL LORD, IT MAY

SEEM HARD TO ME, BUT HE KNOW I CAN HANDLE

IT THAT'S WHY HE PUT ME IN CHARGE

VERY SPECIAL TO HIM, NO MATTER WHAT

WAIT... THAT'S WHAT HE BEING DOING FOR ALL OF US

X OUT THE DEVIL... AND HE WILL FLEE, YOU WILL SEE

WHY I SAY FROM A TO Z ALL THE

BLESSINGS JESUS HAS DONE FOR ME!

My Life was Spared

I COULD OF LOSTED MY LIFE… ON HALLOWEEN NIGHT, THE DEVIL WANTED ME DEAD BUT GOD SAID… MY CHILD WILL LIVE, THIS ONE YOU NOT GONE KILL!!!!! AND IT HAPPENED SO FAST, THE DEVIL PLANNED THE CRASH, DIDN'T HAVE TIME TO PRAY, DIDN'T HAVE TO THINK, ALL I KNOW IS MY HEART DID SINK !!! BUT RIGHT NOW TODAY, IM THANKFUL THAT THERE IS A GOD, AND HE SAVED ME FROM DYING, AND MY FAMILY FROM CRYING, OF PAIN AND SORROW, I'M SO THANKFUL I CAN SEE TOMORROW, I KNOW I CAN SAY THE LORD LOVES ME… IT WASN'T IN HIS WILL, IT WASN'T IN HIS PLAN, FOR ME TO DIE BY THE DEVIL HAND!! THE DEVIL COULDN'T TOUCH ME AS YOU CAN SEE, I GOT OUT WITH NO CUTS, KNOTS, OR BRUISES, SO DEVIL FLEE, BECAUSE THE LORD IS WITH ME… BUT I AM SO HAPPY AND THANK FUL TO BE LOVED BY THE BEST, BUT I KNOW THE THINGS WE GO THROUGH IS ONLY A TEST… HE LET

ME LIVE SO I CAN TELL THE WORLD... THAT HE IS
REAL, AND HE GAVE ME A SECOND CHANCE SO I CAN
SAY THANK YOU JESUS ANOTHER DAY, I TAKE TIME TO
PRAY MORNING, NOON, AND NIGHT, AND IT'S A GOOD
THING I DO, BECAUSE THAT COULD HAVE BEEN THE
END OF MY FLIGHT, MY SUBWAY TO ETERNITY.... I WAS
HEADED IN THE RIGHT DIRECTION, BUT TO LIVE IS
SUCH A BLESSING, YOU NEED TO BE THANKFUL FOR
EVERY BREATH YOU BREATHE, LIFE MIGHT NOT BE
A BOWL OF CHERRIES, BUT IT'S A HEART BREAKER
WHEN YOU LEAVE!! SO ENJOY AND BE THANKFUL
EVERYDAY... BECAUSE SOME PEOPLE DON'T HAVE THE
CHANCE TO PRAY, THE LORD BLESSED ME, AND HE
WILL DO THE SAME FOR YOU, BUT ITS YOUR CHOICE
YOU HAVE TO CHOOSE, LIVE FOR THE LORD, DON'T BE
MISLEADED, OR OF COURSE YOU SHOULD KNOW THE
DIRECTION YOUR HEADED...... BUT IF YOU NOT EVEN
TRYING TO KNOW THE LORD, THE DEVIL WILL GET
YOU IN A BLINK OF An EYE, HE WILL TRAP YOU, KEEP
YOU SINNING, LEAD YOU WRONG UNTIL YOU DIE!!! HE
WILL TRAP YOU LIKE HE TRIED TO TRAP ME.... BUT
FOR MY LIFE MY LORD HOLDS THE KEY.... BUT DO YOU
KNOW WHO HOLDS THE KEY.... TO WHERE YOU WILL
SPEND ETERINTY!

God Don't Put More on You.... Then You Can't Bear!

GOD DON'T PUT MORE ON YOU THEN YOU CANT BEAR, IF IT'S TO HARD FOR YOU IT WONT BE THERE, HE KNOW WHAT YOU CANT HANDLE, HE KNOW WHAT YOU CAN, HE KNOWS BECAUSE HE THE MAN WITH THE PLAN. THINGS MIGHT SEEM BAD, BUT THEY WILL GET BETTER, STOP DWELLING ON THE PAST, LIVE FOR TODAY YOUR WORRIES WON'T LAST, JUST GET READY FOR WHAT'S AHEAD, BECAUSE WHEN YOUR TROUBLES ARE OVER... THE BLESSINGS BEGIN!!!! YOU ALWAYS GO THROUGH THE WORST, TO MAKE IT TO THE BEST, BUT DON'T GIVE UP THIS IS ONLY A TEST! THANK GOD FOR THE HARD, IT'S NOT DOING NOTHING BUT MAKING YOU STRONG, AND NOTHING IS TOO HARD FOR THE LORD... ALL YOU HAVE TO DO IS HOLD ON....HE WANNA SEE HOW MUCH FAITH DO YOU HAVE, HOW LONG WILL YOU BELIEVE,

COUNT ON HIM, HE IS THE ONE THAT WILL NEVER
LEAVE! YOU THINK IT'S HARD WHAT'S HAPPENING
TO YOU, BUT DON'T REALIZE WHAT THE NEXT MAN
IS GOING THROUGH…YOU MAY THINK YOUR LIFE
HARDER THEN THE NEXT… BUT REMEMBER… THE
HARDER IT IS …. THE MORE YOU GONE GET BLESSED,
YOU CAN HANDLE IT, YOU JUST DON'T WANT TO,
LET THE LORD HANDLE YOUR PROBLEMS, DON'T
LET YOUR PROBLEMS HANDLE YOU!! DON'T FROWN,
DON'T HOLD YOUR HEAD DOWN… KEEP YOUR HEAD
UP TO THE SKY… KEEP THANKING HIM, DON'T
ASK WHY... THINGS MAY SEEM HARD, BUT DON'T
STOP KEEP GOING. BECAUSE GOD HAS A PLAN, AND
IT CAN'T BE STOPPED BY NO MAN! THE ONLY MAN
CAN STOP YOUR PLAN IS YOU…? YOU THINK HE
TAKING LONG… BUT WHEN IT'S OVER… IT WILL
BE GREAT AND A WONDERFUL BREAK THROUGH …
HE IS NEVER TOO EARLY, HE IS NEVER TO LATE…
PEOPLE AROUND YOU MIGHT BE HAPPY, YOU THINK
LIFE NOT FAIR… BUT JUST ALWAYS KNOW GOD
DON'T PUT MORE ON YOU, THEN YOU CAN BEAR!!!!!

Friends Today Enemies Tomorrow

IT'S A SHAME HOW YOU CAN BE FRIENDS TODAY
AND ENEMIES THE NEXT TIME YOU TURN AROUND,
WHEN YOU THOUGHT THAT PERSON WAS DOWN,
IT'S A SHAME HOW PEOPLE CAN CHANGE IN A WINK
OF A BLINK, JUST BECAUSE A PERSON DON'T THINK,
THAT'S MY HOMIE, THAT'S MY FRIEND, BEEN TRUE
TO ME UNTIL THE END, WHEN I FALL THEY FALL, IF
I CANT SAY NOTHING GOOD ABOUT THEM, IM NOT
GONE SAY NOTHING AT ALL. WHY DO YOU TALK
ABOUT SOMEONE YOU KICK IT WITH EVERYDAY... I
GUESS THEY WASN'T YOUR FRIEND ANYWAY, HOW
CAN YOU SIT UP AND TALK ABOUT A PERSON AFTER
ALL THEY HAVE DONE FOR YOU, BEEN NOTHING
BUT TRUE TO YOU, AND THAT'S THE THANKS WE
GET.... IS BETRAYED IN RETURNED, BEING MY FRIEND
THAT'S SOMETHING YOU HAVE TO EARN... NEVER

TURN YOUR BACK ON GOOD PEOPLE, BECAUSE YOU NEVER KNOW WHEN YOU WILL NEED THEM... YOU MUST BE REAL CRAZY TO TURN YOUR BACK ON THE NEALS... BECAUSE YOU WILL NEVER FIND NO ONE THIS REAL. ALWAYS TALKING ABOUT SOMEBODY..... IS THE BEST YOU CAN DO? ONCE EVERYBODY FIGURE YOU OUT YOU NOT GONE HAVE NO ONE TO TALK TO.... SO FOR ALL YOU BACK STABBING, SNAKES, FAKE, BEGGING AND ALWAYS BORROW.... DON'T SAY YOU MY FRIEND TODAY, BECAUSE I KNOW YOU WILL BE MY ENEMY TOMORROW!

Same Script Different Cast

MEN ARE SOMETHING ELSE THEY PLAY THE SAME OLE GAME… ON DIFFERENT WOMEN, SOME WOMEN DON'T KNOW, SOME WOMEN DO….BUT WE ALL KNOW THEY WANT THEY CAKE AND EAT IT TOO. THE SAME SCRIPT, YOU CANT FOOL ME IM TOO HIP, I KNOW THE GAMES THEY PLAY, I KNOW THE LINES THEY USE, WHEN THEY THINK YOU DON'T KNOW, THEY THINK THEY FOUND THEM SELVES A FOOL, BUT IF A WOMAN BREAK A MAN HEART, THEY WANNA BREAK A LIMB! BUT WE LEARNED FROM THE BEST, WE LEARNED FROM THEM. MEN WANNA RULE THE WORLD AND RUN THINGS, AND TREAT WOMEN LIKE A PUPPET ON A STRING. BUT DON'T LIVE LIKE THAT, US WOMEN NEED TO BE TREATED LIKE QUEENS, BECAUSE WE 'RE THE BEST THING THAT EVER HAPPEN TO MEN, BECAUSE IF IT WASN'T FOR US, THERE WILL BE NO THEM. IF YOU MAKING PLANS FOR THE FUTURE, MAKE SURE THAT MAN

NOT A USER, OR AN ABUSIER A WOMENIZER OR FLIRT BECAUSE IF HE IS YOUR RELATIONSHIP NOT GONE WORK. WHEN HE COME TO YOU, MAKE SURE HE KNOW YOUR STOP IS HIS LAST…. BECAUSE YOU ARE NOT ABOUT TO END UP THE DIFFERENT CAST….

As the Days Go By

I WANNA KNOW WHY….. WHY DO PEOPLE HAVE
TO BE SO CRUEL, AND MEAN, IS IT BECAUSE THEY
THINK THEY DON'T NEED HELP WITH THINGS, WHY
ARE BLACKS AGAINST BLACKS, IS IT BECAUSE THEY
THINK THEY CAN DO THAT. WHY DO PEOPLE HAVE
TO TALK TO PEOPLE WRONG, IS IT BECAUSE THEY
THINK YOU CANT MAKE IT ON YOUR OWN, WHY DO
PEOPLE LEAVE PEOPLE OUT ON A LIMB, IS IT BECAUSE
THEY THINK THEY CAN DO THAT….BECAUSE YOU
NEED THEM. WHY PEOPLE ARE SO SELFISH AND
ONLY THINK ABOUT THEMSELVES, IS IT BECAUSE,
SOMEONE DIDN'T GIVE THEM WHAT THEY NEEDED,
AND THEY COULDN'T GET NO HELP. WHY DO PEOPLE
HAVE TO BE SO DEMANDING, WHEN THEY SHOULD
BE HELPFUL, AND UNDERSTANDING, WHY DO
PEOPLE HAVE TO LOOK DOWN ON YOU, WHEN YOU
OUT THERE DOING WHAT YOU HAVE TO DO. WHY
DO PEOPLE HAVE TO PUT PEOPLE DOWN…….. STOP!!

YOUR LIFE IS MESSED UP TAKE A LOOK AROUND.
PEOPLE THAT ONLY THINK ABOUT THEMSELVES, I
THINK THEY NEED HELP! SOME PEOPLE DON'T EVEN
CARE ABOUT THE KIDS, IT'S SAD IT HAVE TO BE THE
WAY IT IS. AND I PRAY EVERYDAY FOR PEOPLE LIKE
YOU, THAT'S WHAT THE LORD WANT ME TO DO!
"REMEMBER" MY FATHER IN HEAVEN IS WATCHING
YOU. I KEEP MY HEAD TO THE SKY... AND EACH
DAY, AS THE DAYS GO BY...I WANNA KNOW WHY?

Why Do We

WHY DO WE SAY WE HATE DEATH, BUT WE KEEP ON
KILLING, WHY DO WE SAY WE HAVE A HEART, BUT
WE HAVE NO FEELINGS? WHY DO WE SAY WE MISS
YOU, BUT WE ALWAYS STAY AWAY, WHY DO WE SAY
WE NEED HELP, BUT WE NEVER TAKE THE TIME TO
PRAY... WHY DO WE SAY WE HATE SPENDING MONEY,
WHEN MONEY IS MADE TO BE SPENT? WHY DO WE SAY
WE WANT OUR OWN PLACE, BUT WE HATE PAYING
RENT? WHY DO WE SAY WE DON'T WANNA GO TO
JAIL, BUT WE ALWAYS SET OUR SELF UP FOR IT.? WHY
DON'T WE GO TO CHURCH, BUT A CLUB NIGHT WE
WONT MISS...? WHY DO WE ALWAYS SPEAK FIRST,
BUT NEVER THINK BEFORE WE SPEAK...? WHY DO WE
KNOW DRINKING BAD BUT WE ALWAYS DRINK...? WHY
DON'T WE LIKE A GUN USED ON US, BUT WE QUICK
TO PULL THE TRIGGER... BUT U SAY LIFE IS HARD
HOW U FIGURE,WHY DO PEOPLE SAY THEY DON'T
WANNA DIE FROM AIDS, BUT SLEEPING AROUND WITH

NO PROTECTION THESE DAYS... "HELLO" WHY DO WE BELIEVE EVERYTHING WE HEAR, THEN WE TELL IT TO THE NEXT LISTENING EAR. WHY DO WE HATE ON PEOPLE THAT'S DOING GOOD, IS IT BECAUSE YOU THINK YOU CANT, TRY IT!!! YOU COULD... WHY ARE WE ALWAYS IN A HURRY, WHEN THERE'S REALLY NO RUSH, WHY DON'T WE LIKE WAITING, WHEN PATIENCE IS A MUST...? WHY DON'T WE BELIEVE IN GOD, MAN DIDN'T MAKE THE SUN, BY THE WAY WHERE DO YOU THINK YOU CAME FROM? WHY DO WE JUDGE PEOPLE BY A LOOK OR WHAT WE HEAR FROM OTHERS, DIDN'T YOUR MOM EVER TEACH YOU, TO NEVER JUDGE A BOOK BY IT'S COVER... WHY ARE WE JUDGING, WHEN THE REAL JUDGEMENT IS IN THE END. WHY WE SAY WE DON'T TRUST NO ONE, BUT CALL EVERYONE A FRIEND..... WHY DO WE ALWAYS ASK WHY, WHY CAN'T WE LET IT BE, IT'S GONE ALWAYS BE HATING, CONFUSION, GOSSPING, BACK STABBING, HURT, PAIN, AND MISERY... BEING A PART OF IT ... WHY DO WE?

Jesus Spared They Life

THEY COULD OF LOSTED THEY LIFE ON A WET
SUNDAY NIGHT, THE DEVIL WANTED THEM DEAD,
BUT GOD SAID, MY CHILDREN WILL LIVE… THIS
FAMILY YOU NOT GONE KILL!!! BECAUSE IT'S NOT IN
MY WILL!! AND IT HAPPENED SO FAST, THE DEVIL
PLANNED THE CRASH, BUT IT WASN'T A SUCCESS,
BECAUSE WE ARE PROTECTED BY THE BEST!!!
EVERYTHING HAPPEN FOR A REASON, THIS IS ONLY
A TEST. IM THANKFUL THERE IS A GOD, BECAUSE HE
SAVED THEM FROM DYING, OUR FAMILY FROM CRYING,
FROM PAIN AND SORROW, WE ARE SO THANKFUL
THEY ARE HERE, TO SEE TOMORROW… I KNOW THAT
I CAN SAY THE LORD LOVE THEM, BECAUSE IT WASN'T
IN HIS WILL, IT WASN'T IN HIS PLAN, FOR MY FAMILY
TO DIE BY THE DEVIL HANDS! THE DEVIL COULDN'T
TOUCH THEM AS YOU CAN SEE, BECAUSE THEY
WALKED AWAY WITH ONLY CUTS AND BRUISES!!! SO
DEVIL FLEE, BECAUSE GOD GET THE VICTORY!! THEY

DIDN'T LOSE THEY LIFE, THEY DIDN'T LOSE A LIMB,
GOD IS GOOD, PEOPLE NEED TO ALWAYS THANK HIM!
THE DEVIL WORKING! BUT THE LORD WORKING
TOO!!! JESUS IS LOVE, THAT'S WHY HE THERE FOR YOU.
YOU NEED TO BE THANKFUL FOR EVERY BREATH YOU
BREATHE, LIFE MIGHT NOT BE A BOWL OF CHERRIES,
BUT THE GRAVE IS NOT WHERE NOBODY WANNA BE!!
HAVE A RELATIONSHIP WITH GOD AND BE THANKFUL
EVERYDAY, BECAUSE THINGS HAPPEN SO FAST, YOU
DON'T HAVE TIME TO PRAY. GOD SAVED THEM, HE
GAVE THEM A SECOND CHANCE, BECAUSE FOR THEM
HE HAS PLANS. THE DEVIL WANTED TO SEE THEM
LAYING IN A HOSPITAL BED, HALFWAY DEAD, BUT GOD
SAID " LET MY CHILDREN GO " ALL THE ANGELS THAT
WAS AROUND THEM GOT A SIGN FROM ABOVE, AND
HELD ON TIGHT, BECAUSE THE DEVIL WONT MAKE
THIS THEY LAST FLIGHT!! WHEN GOD KEEP YOU
HERE, YOU GOT WORK TO DO, PEOPLE DIE IN A BLINK
OF AN EYE… IT COULD HAVE BEEN YOU. EVERYBODY
WALKED AWAY WITH A SMILE ON THEY FACE, BECAUSE
OF JESUS LOVE AND GRACE!! THEY COULD HAVE DIED
THAT NIGHT, BUT JESUS SAID NO!! AND SPARED THEIR
LIFE!

Never Question God

PEOPLE ALWAYS SAYING WHY GOD LET THIS HAPPEN?
WHY GOD WHY? YOU SHOULD NEVER QUESTION GOD,
HOW YOU GONE QUESTION SOMEONE YOU DON'T
KNOW, HOW COULD YOU QUESTION HIM BUT CAN'T
LIVE FOR HIM, "MAYBE HE SHOULD QUESTION YOU"
WHY DO YOU DO THE THINGS YOU DO, WHY IS IT
SO HARD FOR YOU TO LIVE FOR HIM, WHY ARE YOU
SO BLIND THAT YOU CANT SEE THAT THE DEVIL
IS THE ENEMY, THE LORD IS TRYING TO LEAD YOU
RIGHT, BUT YET YOU WANNA LIVE THE SINFUL LIFE,
WHY DON'T YOU GIVE HIM YOUR ALL AND ALL, BUT
WHY WHEN SOMETHING HAPPEN THAT'S WHO YOU
CALL, HOW COULD YOU LOVE EVIL, WHY DON'T
YOU SEEK JESUS.. HOW COULD YOU WALK AWAY
FROM SOMEONE WHO CREATED YOU...? HOW COME
YOU CAN'T BELIEVE HE TRUE, HOW DO YOU THINK
YOU LIVE EVERYDAY? IF YOU DON'T BELIEVE IN HIM
WHY DO YOU PRAY, WHY DO YOU QUESTION GOD,
YOU HAVE SOME NERVE, WHEN YOU DON'T EVEN

READ HIS WORD, THINGS HAPPEN THE WAY THEY DO TO OPEN YOUR EYES, BECAUSE IT COULD HAVE BEEN YOU. GOD IS GETTING MAD, BUT BAD IS NOT IN HIS PLAN, GOD IS GIVING YOU A SECOND CHANCE, INSTEAD OF QUESTIONING HIM.... YOU NEED TO BE ASKIN FOR FORGIVENESS, YOU SHOULDN'T PLAY WITH THE LORD, BECAUSE HE'S IN CHARGE! AND HE'S COMING BACK, SO YOU SHOULD' NT LET DOWN YOUR GUARD! GOD IS GOOD, GOOD CANT GO ON FOR LONG, BECAUSE IF EVERYTHING BE GOOD, YOU WOULDN'T HAVE TO CALL ON THE LORD, THIS WORLD CANT BE GOOD, BECAUSE IT HAVE TOO MUCH HATE, GOD IS LETTING YOU KNOW IT'S ALMOST TOO LATE...... IF YOU READ HIS WORD YOU WOULD HAVE KNEW ITS GONE GET WORST! BECAUSE THE READERS KNOW IT SAID IT IN THE BIBLE FIRST... THIS IS ONLY THE BEGINNING YOU HAVEN'T SEEN NOTHING YET, YOU BETTER GET IT TOGETHER, SO YOU WONT HAVE TO LIVE THROUGH THAT! SO STOP QUESTIONING GOD, AND START THANKING HIM, BUT JUST TO LET YOU KNOW THAT KILLING, STEALING, DESTROYING, IS THE DEVIL JOB! NOT GOD! SO YOUR BEST BET IS NOT TO QUESTION GOD... BUT TO QUESTION YOURSELF, AND THE QUESTION IS...... WHEN JESUS COME TO TAKE HIS PEOPLE... AM I GONE GET LEFT?

Independent Women

AN INDEPENDENT WOMAN DON'T NEED NO HELP,
SHE CAN HANDLE THINGS ALL BY HERSELF, AN
INDEPENDENT WOMAN DON'T WAIT ON NOBODY,
OR CALL ON NO MAN, BUT IF HE WANNA HELP... HE
CAN, AN INDEPENDENT WOMAN GONE TAKE CARE
OF HOME, SHE DON'T CARE IF SHE HAVE TO DO A
LONE, AN INDEPENDENT WOMAN DON'T NEED NO
HELP, THE ONLY THING YOU CAN DO... IS GET OUT
THE WAY AND HELP YOURSELF. BECAUSE HALF OF
THE TIME YOU CANT AFFORD ME AND MINE, THAT'S
WHY IM NOT ABOUT TO WAIST NO TIME,ON A JOKE
LIVING OFF OF HOPE, IN LIFE CANT COPE,READY
TO RUN, CANT HANDLE NONE,OF THE THINGS AN
INDEPENDENT WOMAN CAN... THAT'S WHY YOU
HAVE TO BE CAREFUL WHEN YOU PICK YOUR MAN...
BECAUSE ANYBODY CAN DO BAD BY THEYSELF... I
DON'T NEED NO HELP TO BRING ME DOWN, IF YOU
CAN'T HANDLE MORE THEN ME, YOU DON'T NEED TO

BE AROUND... I DON'T NEED NO ONE TO TAKE CARE
OF ME AND MINE, BECAUSE BY MYSELF IM DOING
FINE! I GOT IT GOING ON, ON MY OWN, BECAUSE IM
INDEPENDENT, THIS INDEPENDENT WOMAN STAND
OUT FROM ALL THE REST, AND IF YOU CANT HANDLE
MY WORST YOU NOT GETTING MY BEST! AND IF YOU
CAN HANDLE MORE THEN ME YOU CAN KEEP ON
COMING, BUT JUST KNOW IM GONE ALWAYS BE AN
INDEPENDENT WOMAN!

Something I Have to Say

THIS IS SOMETHING I HAVE TO SAY GOD WILL MAKE
A WAY OUT OF NO WAY! ALL YOU HAVE TO DO IS
BELIEVE AND PRAY THE BATTLE IS NOT YOURS IT'S
THE LORDS LIVE FOR HIM HE IS IN CHARGE JUST
THINK ABOUT IT GOD HAS BEEN SO GOOD AS WE CAN
SEE. WE ALL ARE LIVING TESTIMONIES "SHE" WAS IN
A COMA, IN A HOSPITAL BED, AND WHAT THE DOCTOR
SAY SHE WILL NEVER WALK, SHE COULD BARELY
TALK, BLIND AND WILL NEVER MOVE HER LEFT SIDE
GUESS WHAT? THE DEVIL LIED! THINGS HAPPEN
FOR A REASON, GET THE HINT... "T" AND HER KIDS
WAS IN A CAR ACCIDENT... THE CAR GONE BUT THEY
STILL HERE, THEY GOT HIT BY TWO 18 WHEELERS...
AND THE "DEVIL WAS THINKING "KILL"BUT GOD
HAVE THE FINAL SAY... AND IT WASN'T IN GOD WILL...
THEY GOT A CHANCE TO WALK AWAY... THANK GOD
AND PRAY... THIS IS SOMETHING I HAVE TO SAY... THE
DOCTOR SAID BAD THINGS ABOUT "BIGMAN", ONCE

AGAIN IN WASN'T IN GOD PLANS!!! TAKE A LOOK AND SEE HE IS AS HEALTHY AS CAN BE… GOD GAVE US "DAD" THE FAMILY MAN… HE RAISED HIS KIDS AND GRAND KIDS THE BEST THAT HE CAN… HE TAUGHT US AND HE TAUGHT US RIGHT. HE SAID FAMILY SHOULD STICK TOGETHER, AND RIGHT ABOUT NOW OUR FAMILY IS STRONGER AND CLOSER THEN EVER! THE LORD IS GOOD IT'S TIME TO GO HIS WAY, THIS IS SOMETHING I HAVE TO SAY… NOW "MOM" IN THE HOSPITAL… FOR HER THIS IS A TURN AROUND, GOD SAID IT'S TIME TO SETTLE DOWN! THINGS HAPPEN FOR A REASON NOW YOU SEE… WE ALL BEEN PRAYING FOR A BREAKTHROUGH NOW "BLACK CHERRY" IS FINALLY SET FREE! IT'S TIME FOR CHANGE FOR US ALL, BUT IT'S UP TO US WE HAVE TO MAKE THE CALL, GOD NOT GONE BEG, HE JUST GONE STAND THERE AND WAIT… BUT TIME IS WRAPPING UP… ONE DAY IT MIGHT BE TO LATE… GOD SAID COME TO HIM HE WILL LET YOU IN… PRAY FOR FORGIVENESS, HE WILL FORGIVE YOUR SINS… TOMORROW NOT PROMISED SO MAKE IT RIGHT TODAY… SOME PEOPLE DON'T GET A SECOND CHANCE… THIS IS SOMETHING I HAD TO SAY!

You Know You are a Child of God When...

WHEN SOMETHING HAPPEN SO BAD AND THE
DOCTOR THINK NOTHING BUT THE WORST.... BUT
YOU KNOW YOU ARE IN GOOD HANDS.... IF GOD IS
YOUR DOCTOR OR YOUR NURSE.... WHEN THEY SAY
THINGS GONE BE ONE WAY.... GOD CAN TURN THEM
AROUND..... YOU KNOW YOU ARE A CHILD OF GOD
WHEN GOD DON'T LET YOU DOWN... GOD IS YOUR
MEDICINE WHEN YOU FEEL PAIN.... HE'S ONE HOLLER
AWAY... JUST CALL HIS NAME... THINGS MAY SEEM BAD,
BUT HE WILL MAKE IT BETTER.... YOU HAVE TO BE
STILL SIT BACK AND LET HIM!!! YOU KNOW YOU ARE
A CHILD OF GOD WHEN YOU NEARLY DEAD AND GOD
PULL YOU THROUGH.... NOW YOU ARE A WALKING
TESTIMONY, YOU HAVE WORK TO DO, SOULS TO SAVE,
TELL PEOPLE WHAT HAPPENED TO YOU!! NO GUN
CAN KILL IF IT'S NOT IN THE LORDS WILL, THINGS

CAN HAPPEN TO ANYBODY YOUNG, OLD, GOOD, OR BAD... AND IT'S SAD THAT THE WORLD IS THE WAY IT IS.... YOU WILL MAKE IT, AS LONG AS YOU ARE A CHILD OF HIS...NOTHING IS IMPOSSIBLE, NOTHING IS TOO HARD, YOU ALL GOOD AS LONG AS YOU GOT THE LORD!!! HE WILL TURN EVERYTHING WRONG, INTO EVERYTHING WONDERFUL, YOUR PAIN INTO PRAISE, YOUR PAST INTO PEACE, YOUR LOST INTO LOVE... JUST LOVE HIM UP ABOVE... AND HE WILL SHOW YOU BETTER THEN I CAN TELL YOU... IF YOU WANNA BE ON THE TEAM THAT'S GONE WIN... "STOP"!! AND ASK THE LORD TO FORGIVE YOU FROM YOUR SINS.... AND MEAN IT FROM THE BOTTOM OF YOUR HEART ... AND YOUR NEW LIFE WILL START. YOU WILL BE NOTHING BUT HAPPY, NOTHING BUT BLESSED, NOTHING BUT PEACE, LOVE AND JOY,AND YOUR MIND WILL BE AT REST, NO STRESS...YOU WILL HAVE A NEW OUTLOOK ON LIFE, IT DON'T MATTER WHERE YOU CAME FROM, YOU STILL CAN BE A CHOSEN ONE.WHEN YOU DO WRONG, AND YOU FEEL KIND OF ODD.. THAT'S WHEN YOU KNOW YOU DON'T BELONG WITH THAT CROWD. BECAUSE YOU ARE A CHILD OF GOD!

Death Clock

THREE HUNDRED SIXTY FIVE DAYS OF THE YEAR.....
WE ALL DON'T EVEN KNOW WHY WE ARE HERE, WE
DON'T KNOW IF OUR TIME FAR OR NEAR, ARE WE
HERE LIVING JUST TO DIE, PEOPLE DIE ALL KIND
OF WAYS, AND NONE OF US KNOW WHEN IS OUR
DAY, OR HOW, WHAT AGE OR WHAT TIME, BUT WE
ALL KNOW ONE DAY WE DYING. YEA YOU SAY IT'S
SCARY, BUT IT'S NOT THAT SCARY, YOU NOT THAT
WORRIED, YOU KNOW WHAT TO DO,DON'T ACT
LIKE NOBODY BROUGHT IT TO YOU... EVERYBODY
KNOW DEATH IS REAL........ BUT YOU PLAYNG WITH
LIFE.... LIKE THIS IS MY LIFE LET ME LIVE..... YOU
GONE LIVE ALRIGHT UNTIL IT COME TO AN END....
AND AFTER DEATH... THE AFTER LIFE BEGIN...
"ETERNAL" DON'T KNOW IF IT'S PEACE OR BURNING!!!
HAVE YOUR FUN THINKING IT CANT HAPPEN TO
YOU.... IT HAPPENED TO SOMEBODY YOU KNOW,
WHAT MAKE YOU THINK YOU CANT GO!! WHEN

YOU WAKE UP REALIZE YOU DEAD!!!! YOU GONE BE
THINKING "OH YEH" IT'S TRUE!! NOW WHAT DO
I DO!! YOUR FIRST LIFE IS THROUGH.... IM SORRY
FOR YOU!!! FROM JANUARY THUR DECEMBER HOW
MANY PEOPLE YOU KNOW DIED, DO YOU REMEMBER?
YOU COULD BE NEXT, I COULD BE TO, IF WE ARE
CAREFUL OR NOT, TIME DON'T WAIT, IF IT'S TIME
YOUR HEART WILL STOP!!! LIFE IS NOT A GAME, THE
DEATH CLOCK IS TICKING!!!! ARE YOU LISTENING?
EVERYONE HAVE THEY OWN LIFE AND DEATH
CLOCK.... IS YOUR CLOCK ABOUT TO STOP!!! TIC TOC

Pray

THE WORD FOR TODAY IS GOD IS GOOD... HE'S SO
GOOD WORDS CAN'T EXPLAIN.... HE LOVE YOU SO
MUCH HE WILL TAKE AWAY YOUR PAIN, THERE'S NO
NEED TO WORRY, THERE'S NO NEED TO FRET, IF A
PERSON DON'T KNOW JESUS, A PERSON HAVEN'T
MET THE BEST. EVERYDAY YOU HAVE A REASON TO
BE HAPPY AND SMILE, IF GOD IS FOR US WHO CAN
BE AGAINST US, THANK GOD FOR ALL YOUR TRIALS,
BECAUSE GOD LOVE YOU MORE THEN YOU CAN
THINK. HE'S THERE AND CARE AND THE LORD DON'T
PUT NOTHING ON YOU THEN YOU CAN BEAR. DON'T
LOOK DOWN, DON'T FROWN, YOU MIGHT CAN'T SEE
HIM, BUT HE IS AROUND... ALL YOU HAVE TO DO IS
GIVE GOD YOUR BEST, AND HE IS SO MERCIFUL HE
WILL DO THE REST. BUT I AM HERE JUST TO SAY.....
JESUS CAN MAKE A WAY OUT OF NO WAY, ALL U HAVE
TO DO IS BELIEVE, TRUST, HAVE FAITH, AND PRAY!

Dead Beat Dads

TO ALL THE MEN IN THE WORLD WHO DON'T CARE….
THIS IS FOR YOU SO BE AWARE. SOME MEN DON'T CARE
ABOUT A THING, WANNA PARTY AND ACT WILD CANT
EVEN TAKE CARE OF THERE CHILD, I DON'T CARE IF
IT'S 1, IF IT'S 2, OR IF IT'S 3, IF YOU CANT TAKE CARE
OF YOUR CHILD, YOUR NOT A FATHER TO ME… WHY
DO SOME MEN WANNA MAKE A CHILD, BUT DON'T
WANNA MAKE THAT CHILD LIFE WORTH WHILE….
IT'S NOT ONLY ABOUT BUYING THINGS, IT'S ABOUT
A HUG, IT'S ABOUT ATTENTION, IT'S ABOUT LOVE…
MEN NEED TO SHOW THERE KIDS THE WORLD, IT
SHOULDN'T MATTER IF IT'S A BOY OR A GIRL… SHOW
THEM THINGS, YOU HAVENT SEEN, SHOW THEM LIFE
TREAT THEM RIGHT, THEY NOT ASKING FOR MUCH,
ALL THEY NEED IS A DADDYS TOUCH! SPENDING TIME
WITH YOUR KIDS THAT WON'T STOP YOUR LIFE, IF
YOU THINK ABOUT IT, IT WILL MAKE IT RIGHT….
CHILDREN DON'T ASK TO BE BORN, THEY DON'T

MEAN NO HARM, AND YOU CAN'T GET MAD BECAUSE
YOU HAVE TO PAY THE COST, YOU CANT GET MAD
AT THE KIDS IT'S NOT THEY FAULT! WHY YOU OUT
THERE MAKING MONEY SPENDING IT LIKE CRAZY, I
WONDER HOW YOU FEEL WHEN YOU DON'T SPEND IT
ON YOUR BABY? DEAD BEAT DADS MAKE ME MAD, AND
THINKING ABOUT MAKE ME SAD, DEAD BEAT DADS
ARE A DISGRACE, AND THEY CANT GET MAD TO FIND
ANOTHER MAN TAKING THEY PLACE, ALL THEY CAN
DO IS LOOK CRAZY AND GET READY….. FOR WHEN
THEY CHILD CALL THE NEXT MAN DADDY!

Congratulation

CONGRATULATION TO A FATHER, A MAN YOUR
CHILD CAN CALL DADDY, GIVE THE MAN HIS PROPS...
YOU KNOW, THE CHILD KNOW, AND HE KNOW,
HE CARE…. CONGRATULATION TO A MAN THAT
KNOW HOW TO MAKE A BABY AND RAISE ONE TO, I
BET A DEAD BEAT DAD BEEN A FATHER FOR YEARS,
AND RAISING A CHILD TO HIM THAT'S NEW. cHE
SUPPOSE TO BE THERE AND HE'S NOT, AND THAT'S
WHEN A REAL MAN COME IN AND TAKE THAT
SPOT. CONGRATULATION TO A MAN, WHO TAKE
A FATHERLESS CHILD IN HIS ARMS, PROTECT HIM
FROM HARM, AND GIVE THAT CHILD A HUG, AND
SHOW HIM MUCH LOVE…. FOR REAL FATHERS I PRAY,
AND WHEN I SEE THEM THEY GET MUCH LOVE AND
RESPECT THIS WAY! EVERY CHILD NEED A MOMMY
AND A DADDY IN THERE LIFE, IF ONE PARENT MISSING
THAT'S NOT RIGHT, CHILDREN ARE LOVEABLE AND
IF THAT CHILD NOT IN YOUR LIFE, YOU NEED TO GO

ADD THAT PIECE TO THAT PUZZLE! SO YOU AND THAT CHILD LIFE CAN BE COMPLETE. THE ONLY EXCUSE THAT YOU CAN HAVE FOR NOT BEING IN YOUR CHILD LIFE…. IF YOU ARE DECEASED!! CONGRADULATION TO THE FATHERS THAT'S AROUND, AND CONGRATULATION TO THE MOTHERS THAT'S THERE, BECAUSE A LOT OF MOTHERS ARE DEAD BEATS AND DON'T CARE…. IT'S NOT JUST THE MEN, ITS SOME WOMEN TOO, BUT IF YOU TAKE CARE OF YOUR LITTLE ONES….. CONGRATULATION TO YOU!!!

I Am Me

I am who I am that's all I can be, you don't like what you see...
don't look at me I can't look like or be who you want me to be. I
can only look like and be me, I'm not trying to be like the next
person, I'm gone be myself...... I can't live for nobody else. I can't
try to be like everybody and I'm not gone try, if you don't like
me that's your problem... goodbye.. you can't tell me nothing I
already know, if you don't like me and so..! I am me and I know
who I can be, so you or nobody else have no right to judge, this
is my life and everything about me I love! I am too blessed to be
stressed, and people on this earth I am not gone try to impress. I
love me, so you are the one with the problem, and worried about
me, you gone have to do a lot of solving, wondering, and figuring
out... because I'm gone be myself no doubt. I can't live for you, I
can only live for me and mine, so stop worrying about my style,
because I'm happy and doing fine, if god is pleased, I'm happy
so I don't care what you say.. So for inquiring minds, remember
this line; if you try to make everybody happy by doing what
they want you to do, everybody gone be happy except you!

Still Broken

WE ARE HERE FOR REASON, NOT TO PLEASE PEOPLE, BUT TO PLEASE JESUS! PEOPLE ARE IN YOUR LIFE FOR A SEASON...EVENTUALLY THEY ALL JUST PASSING BY... EITHER THEY GONE BE A LESSON OR A BLESSING, WE ARE NOT PUT ON THIS EARTH TO BE JUDGED, WE ARE PUT HERE TO LOVE AND TO BE LOVED IF SOMEONE MAKE U FROWN...BREAK YOUR HEART... PUT U DOWN...MISTREAT YOU...USE YOU...OR ABRUISE YOU...THIS PERSON IS A LESSON... BUT IF THEY LOVE YOU...SHOW YOU LOVE...HUG YOU...AND RESPECT YOU...THIS PERSON IS A BLESSING...YOU CANT LIVE YOUR LIFE HURTING WITH YOUR HELD DOWN, SMILING ON THE OUTSIDE...BUT ON THE INSIDE YOU FROWN...YOU CANT KEEP ALLOWING YOURSELF TO BE MISTREATED, YOU ARE BEAUTIFUL...NO MATTER WHAT...IF THEY CANT TALK TO YOU LIKE A PERSON... THEY NOT WORTH IT...IF THEY CANT ASK YOU HOW YOU DOING, OR HOW YOU FEEL, IT'S NOT REAL... IF

YALL CAN'T COMMUNICATE WITHOUT GETTING
MAD, MOVE ON IT'S ALL BAD...IF THEY SAY HURTFUL
THINGS TO YOU WHEN IN AN ARGUMENT, THEY SAID
IT BECAUSE THAT'S WHAT THEY MEANT...IF THEY
PUT THEY HANDS ON YOU, THEY HAVE CROSSED THE
LINE TO THE POINT OF NO RETURN...THE LINE OF
RESPECT...HAS BEEN CUT, BURIED AND BURNED...
THEY DO WHAT THEY DO...THEN SAY SORRY TO YOU...
SORRY IS NO GOOD HERE,THAT WONT WORK,BECAUSE
AFTER ALL THE SORRY YOU STILL GONE BE HURT...
BECAUSE IF YOU BREAK A GLASS AND SAY IM SORRY
OR I WAS JUST JOKIN...WHAT GOOD IS SORRY GONE
DO,WHEN THAT GLASS IS STILL BROKEN...

Always on Time

HE'S ALWAYS ON TIME, SO YOU SHOULDN'T HAVE
A DOUBT IN YOUR MIND, JUST PRAY AND PRAY
UNTIL YOU CAN'T PRAY NO MORE... HE'S WAITING...
ALL YOU HAVE TO DO IS OPEN THE DOOR... SO
DON'T WALK AROUND SAYING WHY ME, IT'S TO
HARD, I CANT HANDLE IT, AND YOU DON'T CARE,
BECAUSE IT'S A BLESSING AND GOD DON'T PUT
NOTHING ON YOU THAT YOU CANT BEAR!

Who Cares

OUR FAMILY HAS BEEN THROUGH A LOT, BUT A
BLESSING IS COMING IN THE END, WE BEEN HIT
BY A TRUCK, SHOT IN THE HEAD, AND STABBED
BY OUR SO CALLED FRIENDS, WE BEEN LIED ON,
LIED TO, USED AND ABRUISED, WE BEEN PLAYED
AND BETRAYED, WE KNOW THE DEAL WE NOT
NO FOOLS. PEOPLE HATE, AND FAKE, SOME NOT
ALL, THEY HATE TO SEE US UP, AND LOVE TO
SEE US FALL, WE BEEN NOTHING BUT GOOD TO
PEOPLE, NOTHING BUT TRUE, WHY DON'T YOU
LIKE US, WHAT HAVE WE DONE TO YOU, WE DON'T
KNOW, WE DON'T CARE, WE NOT TRYING TO
FIGURE IT OUT, THEY SMILE IN OUR FACE, TALK
BEHIND OUR BACK, HOW CAN PEOPLE BE FAKE
LIKE THAT? WE ARE THE SISTER YOU LOVE TO
HATE, WE HAVE A BOND, WE TIGHT, WE REAL, AND
WE CAN NEVER BE FAKE... WE ARE DIFFERENT

JUST KNOW... WE TOO BLESSED TO BE
STRESSED OR DEPRESSED... SO GIVE IT A
REST... IF YOU DON'T LIKE US LET US GO....

Wait There's More..................

IN LIFE FOR YOU.... GOD HAS SO MUCH IN STORE...
BUT YOU DON'T STICK AROUND LONG ENOUGH, TO
LEARN MORE... I KNOW TIMES GET ROUGH, THINGS
GET HARD ... BUT WHEN IT GET LIKE THAT, THAT'S
THE ONLY TIME YOU CALL ON THE LORD... YOU
SHOULD THANK HIM EVERYDAY... IN EVERYHING
YOU DO PRAY... BECAUSE GOD WILL MAKE A WAY
OUT OF NO WAY... WHY YOU THINK YOU HERE
ANOTHER DAY? GOD HAS SO MUCH PLANNED FOR
YOU... YOU HAVE NO IDEA... HOW AMAZING HE IS...
YES HE'S REAL! BUILD A RELATIONSHIP... TELL HIM
HOW YOU FEEL, OPEN UP YOUR HEART AND THAT'S
A START... TO LIVING FOR HIM... WE NEED HIM
EVERY MIN... EVERY SECOND, EVERY HOUR, IF YOU
CAN'T ADMIT TO THAT YOU ARE A COWARD... DON'T
WORRY ABOUT THEM, BECAUSE WE ARE NOTHING
WITHOUT HIM... WE ARE LOSTED ON THE ROAD TO
DESTRUCTION...EVERYTIME YOU PICK UP THE BIBLE

YOU RUSHING... TAKE YOUR TIME AND GET TO KNOW YOUR CREATOR... HE WILL FORGIVE YOU HE CAN'T HATE US ... ONE DAY AT TIME, TAKE A DIFFERENT STEP EVERYDAY ... BUT IN ALL THINGS PRAY! KEEP YOUR HEAD UP TO THE SKY... DON'T QUESTION GOD, DON'T ASK WHY... LEAN NOT UNTO YOUR OWN UNDERSTANDING... TRUST IN GOD FOR YOU HE'S PLANNING... KEEP IN TOUCH DON'T GIVE UP... HANG AROUND FOR YOU HE HAVE SO MANY THINGS IN STORE... WAIT WHERE YOU GOING, THERE'S MORE

To My Beautiful Sister

TO MY SISTER MY FRIEND, YOU ARE A WONDERFUL PERSON, YOU WILL HOLD IT DOWN UNTIL THE END. YOU ARE A GREAT MOTHER, YOU DON'T PLAY NO GAMES, YOU DON'T TELL NO FAIRYS, AND YOU ARE ONE PERSON THAT DON'T GET WORRIED, AND WILL TAKE CARE OF YOUR FAMILY BY ANY MEANS NECESSARY!! YOU WORK HARD, YOU INDEPENDENT, AND YOU ARE STRONG... YOU GO GIRL YOU GOT IT GOING ON!! YOU SPEAK POSITIVE EVERYDAY, YOU ALRIGHT WITH ME TONYA LASHAY... YOU ARE MY SISTER AND I LOVE YOU SO, AND IM NEVER GOING TO LET YOU GO.... WE HAVE A SISTER BOND THE WORLD WILL NEVER KNOW... THIS IS TO MY BIG SISTER, STAY TRUE, KEEP DOING WHAT YOU DO, AND I WILL ALWAYS LOVE YOU!!!!

Take Care... and Careless...

TAKE CARE AND CARELESS... THESE DAYS TAKE CARE
OF YOURSELF, WORRY ABOUT YOU... WHO CARES
WHAT OTHER PEOPLE WANNA DO, WHO CARES WHAT
THEY THINK ABOUT YOU.... IF THEY NEGATIVE,
LEAVE THEM WHERE THEY STAND... THEY OPINION
DON'T MATTER... FOR THEY OWN LIFE THEY DON'T
HAVE PLANS... DON'T WORRY ABOUT THE PAST
ANYTHING THAT'S BACK THERE, IT'S A REASON IT'S
BEHIND... LIVE FOR TODAY BE STRESS AND WORRY
FREE ... BE HAPPY WITH YOURSELF BE YOU AND YOU
WILL SEE... THE OLD SHOULD BE BURIED ... DON'T
LET NO ONE WORRIES BECOME YOUR WORRIES...
WHO CARES WHAT PEOPLE SAY? WHO ARE THEY TO
JUDGE? GOD ABOVE IS THE ONLY JUDGE YOU CANT
CHANGE NO ONE, THERE'S NO NEED TO TRY.... DONT
WORRY ABOUT IT .... DON'T ASK WHY... JUST BE
YOURSELF IS THE BEST PERSON TO BE... LOVIN YOU
AND BEING FREE... IF THEY NOT TALKING TO YOU,

THEY TALKING ABOUT YOU, LET THEM TALK THEY DOING IT BECAUSE THEY ARE STRESS ... YOU KEEP WALKING AND CARELESS... IF SOMEONE DON'T LIKE YOU IT'S BECAUSE THEY DON'T LIKE THEYSELF... YOU DID YOUR BEST SO CARELESS... IF PEOPLE THROW STONES AT YOU OVER OLD THINGS AND NEW... THEY DON'T HAVE NOTHING ELSE BETTER TO DO... YOU KNOW WHAT YOU DID AND TO NO ONE YOU DON'T HAVE NOTHING TO PROVE... KEEP IT MOVING STAY POSITIVE ON THE RIGHT TRACK IF YALL NOT HANGING OUT NO MORE ... THAT'S GOOD THEY ARE WITH THE RIGHT PACK? LET PEOPLE FIND THEY OWN WAY... ALL YOU DO IS STAY ON TRACK AND PRAY... FOR YOU WILL BE BETTER DAYS... JUST REMOVE ALL THE BITTERNESS, HATE, HURT, PAIN, UNFORGIVENESS, REPLACE IT WITH LOVE, AND FORGIVENESS, YOUR MIND WILL BE AT REST ... TAKE CARE AND CARELESS!

Peeked Into My Future

PEEKED INTO MY FUTURE, AND WHAT DID YOU SEE…
GOD IS BLESSING ME… GOD HAS SO MUCH MORE, IN
MY FUTURE GOD HAS A LOT OF THINGS IN STORE…
THE MORE HE PEEKED THE MORE HE CREEPEED …
BECAUSE HE KNOWS WHEN I TRUST, IN MY HEART,
THERE'S NO ROOM FOR DOUBT… JUST KNOW YOU
ARE ABOUT TO BE BLESSED, WHEN EVERYTHING
AROUND YOU BECOME A MESS… DON'T QUESTION,
DON'T GUESS, JUST KNOW THIS IS A TEST…THANK
GOD AND PRAY, BECAUSE YOUR BLESSING IS ON THE
WAY!!!! DON'T GIVE UP, DON'T QUIT, YOU HAVE A
BLESSING WITH YOUR NAME ON IT… JUST KNOW
WHEN YOUR WORLD COME TUMBLING DOWN, YOUR
HEART IS HURTING, ON YOUR FACE YOU WEAR A
FROWN, JUST KNOW GOD IS RIGHT THERE, ABOUT
TO TURN YOUR LIFE AROUND…. YOU MAY FEEL YOU
ARE AT THE END OF THE ROPE… BUT DON'T LET
GO THERE'S HOPE!! TRUST IS THE KEY… THE MORE

YOU TRUST, THE MORE THE DEVIL WILL FLEE...
THE DEVIL PEEKED INTO YOUR FUTURE... AND HE
GETTING MAD... HE TRY TO KEEP YOU SAD.... HE
WANT YOU TO DOUBT... BECAUSE THE DEVIL KNOW,
GOD IS ABOUT TO SHOW UP AND SHOW OUT.... THE
DEVIL DON'T WANNA SEE YOU SMILE, HE WANNA
SEE YOU DOWN... BUT LOOK UP, BECAUSE YOU ARE
NOT ALONE GOD IS ALWAYS AROUND...THE HARDER
YOU TRY, THE HARDER YOU CRY... ITS SEEM LIKE
NOTHING IS GETTING BETTER AS THE DAYS GO
BY... JUST KNOW THAT GOD CARE, AND JUST KEEP
WALKING FORWARD, YOUR BLESSING IS RIGHT
THERE.... IF YOU'RE GOING THROUGH A TOUGH
TIME IN YOUR LIFE... HOLD ON, BE STRONG, AND
FIGHT.... IN THE END GOD WILL MAKE IT RIGHT....
THE DEVIL MAYBE WORKING, BUT GOD IS WORKING
TOO.... KEEP IN MIND GOD WILL NEVER FAIL YOU....
THE DEVIL PEEKED INTO YOUR FUTURE HE KNOW,
THAT YOUR BLESSINGS ABOUT TO OVER FLOW......
SO KEEP A SMILE ON YOUR FACE IN THE MIST OF IT
ALL... HOLD ON AND DON'T LET GO... HE PEEKED
INTO YOUR FUTURE AND YES HE DID SEE, THAT GOD
ALMIGHTY HAS PLANS FOR YOU AND FOR ME.....

Happy Mother's Day

MOTHER'S ARE FULL OF LOVE, ARMS YOU CAN RUN
TO WHEN YOU NEED A HUG... NEVER LET YOU DOWN,
NEVER JUDGE... WITH A MOTHER YOU CAN GO TO
WHEN FEELING DOWN, A MOTHER KNOWS THE
RIGHT THINGS TO SAY, TURN YOUR FROWN INTO A
SMILE.... A MOTHER LOVE CAN NEVER BE REPLACED, A
MOTHER WILL ALWAYS MAKE AWAY OUT OF NO WAY...
I LOVE YOU MOTHER AND HAPPY MOTHERS DAY!!!!

Life

HELLO MY NAME IS LIFE… I CAN TREAT YOU WRONG OR I CAN TREAT YOU RIGHT… I CAN GIVE YOU UPS, I CAN GIVE YOU DOWNS, I CAN MAKE YOU LAUGH, I CAN MAKE YOU FROWN… YOU CAN BE BLESSED OR YOU CAN BE CURSED … YOU CAN BE AT YOUR BEST OR YOU CAN BE AT YOUR WORST… DO YOU WANNA DEAL YOUR HAND? OR DO YOU WANT ME TO DEAL YOUR HAND FOR YOU… WILL YOU LIVE, LAUGH, LOVE, WILL YOUR LIFE BE A BOWL OF CHERRIES… OR WILL YOUR LIFE BE FULL OF COMPLAIN AND WORRY… I AM LIFE… DO YOU TAKE ME FOR GRANTED? DO YOU USE ME OR ABRUISE ME? DO YOU HURT ME? DO YOU OVER WORK ME? WITHOUT ME THERE'S NO AIR… SO IF YOU TAKE ME FOR GRANTED BEAWARE… IN YOUR HEART DON'T BE BITTER, DON'T HOLD GRUGES, DON'T HATE, DON'T HAVE STRIFE… IT'S YOURS ONLY TEMPORORY… ITS CALLED LIFE…

Let Your Mess... Be Your Message

NO ONE IS PERFECT, FROM THAT WE ARE VERY FAR...
WE MIGHT NOT BE PREFECT BUT IN GOD EYES WE
ARE STARS... IN YOUR LIFETIME YOU ARE GOING TO
HAVE PROBLEMS, AND WORRIES, YOU ARE GOING
TO GO THROUGH LESSONS AND GOD IS GOING TO
SURPRISE YOU WITH MANY BLESSINGS!! SOME DAYS
GONE BE A MESS, SOME DAYS GONE BE YOUR BEST!!
BUT LET YOUR MESS BE YOUR MESSAGE, AND SHARE
WHAT YOU BEEN THROUGH... NOT SO THAT PEOPLE
CAN USE IT AGAINST YOU, BUT TO HELP THEM GET
A BREAK THROUGH.... LET THEM KNOW WHEN IT
RAIN IT POURS, BUT WHILE ITS RAINING PRAY MORE
AND MORE... IT'S NOT GONE RAIN FOREVER, LIFE
IS HARD BUT IT WILL GET BETTER... AND WHEN
THE STORM IS OVER THOSE PROBLEMS END, THE
HORRIBLE CHAPTER OF YOUR LIFE IS CLOSED... A

NEW BEGINNING, BEGIN AGAIN… ONE THING YOU CAN NOT DO! YOU CAN NOT LOOK BACK! IF YOU DO, YOU WILL END UP BACK ON THE WRONG TRACK!!! SO MOVE FORWARD, LOOK AHEAD… AND TELL YOUR WORRIES AND PROBLEMS THAT TO ME… YOU ARE DEAD!! FOR ME GOD HAS SO MUCH MORE!!! JUST LET YOUR TROUBLES GO, THEN GOD WILL LET YOUR BLESSINGS FLOW… DON'T STAY IN THAT MESS!!GIVE GOD YOUR BEST, AND HE WILL DO THE REST… IF YOU THINK ABOUT IT LIFE IS ONLY A TEST… TO SEE HOW LONG YOU CAN STAND STRONG… IN HARD TIMES, HOLD ON GOD ALWAYS COME THROUGH I'M NOT LYING!!! EVERYTHING HAPPEN FOR A REASON, EVERYTHING IS PLANNED, GOD IS BUILDING YOU FOR SOMETHING STRONGER AHEAD, HE'S BUILDING YOUR STRENGTH, HES BUILDING YOUR FAITH, HE'S MOLDING YOU INTO SOMETHING GREAT!!! REMEMBER WE ARE BUILT TO STAND NOT BUILT TO BREAK! THE THINGS WE GO THROUGH IN LIFE IS A LESSON, HELP THE NEXT PERSON, DON'T HOLD IT IN LET YOUR MESS BE YOUR MESSAGE!

Just the 2 of Us

JUST THE TWO OF US ... YOU AND ME, SHE IS
EVERYTHING I HOPED SHE WOULD BE.... SHE IS
VERY SMART, TALENTED IN EVERYTHING SHE DO...
IN SCHOOL HONOR ROLL STUDENT... TOP TEN IN
HER CLASS ... VALADICTORIAN TO, SHE CAN ALSO
DESIGN CLOTHES FOR ME AND YOU... SHE GOT SO
MANY AWARDS, MANGED SO MANY TEAMS... IN HIGH
SCHOOL SHE PRETTY MUCH HELD DOWN A LOT OF
THINGS... SHE WAS ON TV GREAT DAY ST. LOUIS, ON
CHANNEL 4... NOW SHE POSTED UP ON BROADWAY
THANK GOD FOR MY PRIDE AND JOY... SHE MAKE
ME SMILE, SHE MAKE ME PROUD... SHE MAKE ME
KNOW THAT I AM VERY BLESSED... IN COLLEGE
DOING GOOD, IN LIFE DOING GREAT... BEAUTIFUL
YOUNG LADY, WITH A BIG BRIGHT BEAUTIFUL SMILE
ON HER FACE... SHE'S ALWAYS HAPPY GO LUCKY
DON'T LET NOTHING GET HER DOWN... SHE IS
FULL OF JOY... VERY PLAYFUL... THANK GOD THAT

SHE AROUND… SHE VERY RESPECTFUL, SHE VERY
UNIQUE, SHE'S PEACEFUL, SHE LOVE TO SING AND
THAT'S ALRIGHT WITH ME… SHE BELONG TO ME,
GOD SAID HERE'S YOUR CHILD TAKE CARE… ALL I
CAN SAY IS THANK YOU LORD FOR HER… THERE'S
MORE GOD HAVE IN STORE… THIS IS NOT IT…
WHEN GOD WAS PICKING MOTHERS…MAN IM GLAD
I WAS PICKED… I AM PROUD TO SAY I LOVE BEBE
EVERYDAY, THAT'S MY STAR, MY GIRL, MY WORLD….
SHE'S ALL THERE IS TO LIVE FOR… I COULDN'T
ASK FOR MORE… WE SAY WE LOVE EACH OTHER
EVERYDAY… THAT'S A MUST… LIFE IS BEAUTIFUL,
IT'S ALWAYS GONE BE JUST THE TWO OF US.

Get Insured by Chirst

YOU MIGHT HAVE LIFE INSURANCE, YOU MIGHT HAVE CAR INSURANCE, YOU MIGHT HAVE HEALTH INSURANCE, BUT ARE YOU INSURED BY CHIRST? THAT INSURANCE OF ETERNAL LIFE, IT'S FREE JESUS PAID THE PRICE…. AND YOU COVERED FOR THE REST OF YOUR LIFE, HE PAID THE WAY, ALL YOU HAVE TO DO IS STAY LIFTED UP AND PRAY, TRUST, BELIEVE… SIT BACK AND RECEIVE ALL HIS BLESSINGS, STAY STRONG THROUGH ALL HIS LESSONS, EVERYDAY HE IS TESTING…. JESUS IS MY POLICY HOLDER, JESUS IS MY BENEFICIARY, WHEN I LEAVE…. KNOW THAT I'M INSURED BY CHIRST, SO THERES NO NEED TO WORRY!! MY LIFE IS IN HIS HANDS… AND YOURS SHOULD BE, BECAUSE JESUS HOLDS THE KEY TO ETERNITY, EVERYTHING IS GOING TO BE ALRIGHT, GET INSURED BY CHIRST AND KNOW THAT YOU FULL COVERAGE ON YOUR LIFE…. THEN YOU WILL BE IN GOOD HANDS…. LIFE IS SHORT IM NOT PLAYING…

YOUR LIFE CAN BE OVER QUICKER THEN YOU CAN THINK, FASTER THEN YOU CAN BLINK, HERE TODAY, GONE TODAY... GET INSURED BY CHIRST AND PRAY... YOU CAN BE AT EASE, YOUR FAMILY CAN BE RELIEVED. OUR LIVES ARE TEMPORARILY, WE ARE HERE FOR A REASON AND HERE FOR A SEASON... SO LETS GET RIGHT, AND GET INSURED BY CHIRST....

Get Tested/ Be Protected

YOU MIGHT DON'T WANNA TALK ABOUT IT, IF
YOU KNOW A PERSON GOT IT, YOU MIGHT DON'T
WANNA DEAL, READY OR NOT AIDS IS REAL.... A
PERSON CAN SAY THEY LOVE YOU.... AND THEY CAN
BE WALKING AROUND INFECTED!!! THAT'S WHY
YOU MUST ALWAYS BE PROTECTED AND YOU BOTH
GET TESTED!!! SOME MEN OF THIS WORLD.... WILL
NEVER BE SATISFIED, THEY WANNA PROVE A POINT
AND SLEEP WITH EVERY GIRL.... IF HE'S A MAN OF
GOD, HE WILL BE FAITHFUL AND TRUE, BECAUSE IF
HE'S FAITHFUL TO GOD HE WILL BE FAITHFUL TO
YOU... YOU HAVE TO OPEN YOUR EYES, WOMEN LIE
MEN LIE.... THEY WILL TELL YOU ANYTHING TO
GET WHAT THEY WANT, TO GIVE YOU WHAT THEY
GOT, AND IT'S SAD IT HAVE TO BE LIKE THAT....
DON'T BE AFRAID GET TESTED FOR AIDS.... FEAR CAN
MEAN TWO THINGS... FORGET EVERYTHING AND
RUN..... OR FACE EVERYTHING AND RISE.... WHEN

YOU FACE THINGS YOU MAY BE SURPRISED.... DON'T WORRY, FOLLOW GOD HE WILL GUIDE, KEEP YOUR EYES ON GOD..... STRENGTH HE WILL PROVIDE, AND EVERYTHING WILL FALL IN PLACE.... DON'T JUDGE NO ONE JUST KEEP YOUR SELF SAFE.... EVERYONE HAVE TO DIE FROM SOMETHING, BUT DON'T LET IT BE SOMETHING YOU CAN PREVENT... THERES NO RUSH, BE CAREFUL, WHO YOU TRUST, AIDS IS REAL, IT DESTROY'S, IT KILLS... BE WISE OPEN YOUR EYES... IT'S OUT HERE, IT'S TRUE, GET TESTED, BE PROTECTED, IT CAN HAPPEN TO YOU..... LOVE CAN'T PROTECT YOU FROM NO TYPE OF DISEASE.... YOU CAN BE DOING EVERYTHING RIGHT YOU CAN BE FAITHFUL AND TRUE .... DON'T BE SURPRISED AIDS CAN BE SITTING RIGHT NEXT TO YOU.... AND FOR THOSE WHO GOT HIV OR AIDS DON'T DO TO OTHERS WHAT'S BEEN DONE TO YOU...IM SURE IT'S HARD, AND THE WAY THINGS HAPPEN ITS' NOT FAIR.... BUT PASS THE WORD.... SO PEOPLE CAN BE AWARE... AND ALWAYS PUT GOD FIRST, AND YOU WILL NEVER BE LAST, KEEP THE FAITH THIS TOO SHALL PASS!!!

Follow Me...

FOLLOW ME I WILL NEVER LEAVE YOU NOR FORSAKE YOU…YOU HAVE THE CHOICE TO CHOOSE… MY TEAM WINS, THE DEVIL TEAM LOOSE, I WILL PICK U UP WHEN YOU FALL, I ANSWER EVERYTIME YOU CALL, IF YOU LOVE ME GIVE YOUR ALL…. I WILL NEVER TURN MY BACK…. ON ME WHY DO YOU GIVE UP LIKE THAT…? I DIED FOR ALL YOUR SINS… I AM THE BEGINNING AND THE END…. I LOVE YOU NOW AND I LOVED YOU THEN…. EVEN WHEN YOU WAS IN YOUR SIN… IF YOU LOVE ME, DO WHAT I WANT YOU TO…. LIVE FOR ME THAT'S ALL I WANT YOU TO DO…. IT'S NOT HARD TO LIVE FOR THE LORD… STAND STRONG AND DON'T LET DOWN YOUR GUARDS… I WAKE U EVERYDAY, I WATCH YOU WHILE YOU SLEEP, YOU HAVE CLOTHES ON YOUR BACK AND FOOD TO EAT, YOU HAVE A ROOF OVER YOUR HEAD YOU HAVE YOUR HEALTH AND STRENGTH, YOU HAVE MONEY FOR YOUR BILLS YOU HAVE MONEY FOR YOUR RENT….

YOU HAVE LIFE WHY DESTROY IT... AND LIVING FOR
ME WHY AVOID IT... IM ONLY HERE TO SAVE YOUR
SOUL ... THE DEVIL WANT YOU TO LOSE CONTROL OF
YOUR LIFE AND KEEP YOU IN HIS HANDS .... AND FOR
YOU HE HAVE DESTRUCTIVE PLANS.... I HAVE PLANS,
BLESSINGS.... AND ETERNAL LIFE... WALK WITH ME
I CAN MAKE IT RIGHT... REPENT OF YOUR SIN AND
LET'S BEGIN AGAIN... BECAUSE I AM THE ONE AND
ONLY WAY TO HEAVEN THAT YOU CAN GET IN....

Don't Steal

HOW DO IT MAKE YOU FEEL, WHEN YOU
STEAL ...FROM SOME ONE WHO WORK SO HARD TO
BUILD….. YOU TAKE AND THEN YOU MAKE YOUR
SELF…… LOOK BAD…… TAKING WHAT DON'T BELONG
TO YOU IT'S SAD, AND IT MAKE ME VERY MAD…. HOW
CAN YOU LIVE WITH YOURSELF…..? GOING AROUND
BEING A THEIF, IF YOU DON'T HAVE IT YOU DON'T
NEED IT… WORK LIKE ME….. WORK HARD LIKE THE
REST OF THE WORLD, DON'T SIT BACK AND PLOT
ON WHAT SOMBODY ELSE GOT, GET UP AND DO
WHAT YOU HAVE TO DO…. NOT STEAL BUT BUILD,
AND THAT WILL MAKE YOU PROUD OF YOU, YOU
ARE ABLE YOU HAVE HEALTH AND STRENGTH GET
UP AND WORK GET A PLACE PAY SOME RENT, DON'T
GO AROUND TAKING OTHER PEOPLE THINGS… GET
YOUR OWN THE RIGHT WAY IF YOU KNOW WHAT
I MEAN…. YOU SAY IT'S HARD OUT HERE, YEA IT'S
HARD FOR THE ONES THAT'S WORKING TO, AND

YOU MAKE IT HARDER BY DOING WHAT YOU DO…
PEOPLE NEED TO GET IT TOGETHER… PEOPLE NEED
TO MAKE IT BETTER…. DON'T STEAL, DON'T TAKE
IT…. YOU CAN MAKE IT… IT DON'T MATTER IF IT'S
BIG THINGS OR SMALL, IF IT'S NOT YOURS DON'T
TAKE IT AT ALL…. IF SOME ONE TAKE FROM YOU,
YOU WOULDN'T LIKE HOW THAT FEEL…. FROM NOW
ON GET YOUR OWN AND PLEASE DONT STEAL……

Don't Leave Your Family Broken

FAMILY SUPPOSED TO LOVE, HUG, AND TREAT EACH OTHER RIGHT…. RESPECT ONE ANOTHER STAND STRONG ….. LIVE, LAUGH, AND LOVE …. WITH EACH OTHER NOT FIGHT…. THAT'S NOT RIGHT…. FAMILY SHOULD TO BE TIGHT….. DON'T LET THE DEVIL CHANGE YOUR FLIGHT….. WHEN YOU WAS ON THE RIGHT ROAD HE WILL COME IN AND BE VERY BOLD…. HAVE YOU AGAINST YOUR FAMILY HEART SO COLD…. BUT DON'T LET THE DEVIL BREAK THAT STRONG FAMILY BOND…. IT SHOULDN'T BE LIKE THAT, WE ALL WE GOT… FAMILY SHOLUD ALWAYS STICK TOGETHER…. NO MATTER HOW STRONG THE STORM NO MATTER WHAT TYPE OF WEATHER …. LOVE AND PRAYER IS THE KEY AND FAMILY THAT PRAY TOGETHER STAY TOGETHER…. THEN YOU ALL CAN TELL THAT DEVIL TO FLEE…. LOVE ONE ANOTHER EVERYDAY…. IF YOU HAVE ISSUES DON'T HOLD ON TO

IT GO TO THE ONE YOU LOVE AND WORK IT OUT. IF YOU HOLD IT IN TO LONG, WHEN IT DO COME OUT IT'S GONE COME OUT ALL WRONG... FAMILY SHOULD BE ABLE TO FIX IT... NOT JUST LEAVE IT BE.... THE DEVIL WANNA DESTROY WHAT GOD HAS RESTORED LET'S NOT BE ENEMIES..... ASK GOD TO GUIDE, DON'T LET THE DEVIL DIVIDE.... FOLLOW GOD AND YOU WILL SEE... LOVE AND FORGIVE MOVE ON AND LIVE.... FAMILES ARE TOKENS ... IF YOU LOVE YOUR FAMILY DON'T LEAVE IT BROKEN..... YOU HURT YOUR FAMILY, YOU HURT YOURSELF, LIFE IS NOT THE SAME IT FEELS LIKE DEATH..... TAKE TIME PRAY AND TAKE A DEEP BREATH.... GOD IS ALL WE NEED AND FAMILY IS ALL WE HAVE LEFT.... GOD GAVE US EACH OTHER FOR A REASON.... WE ARE HERE ONLY FOR A SEASON..... SO LOVE, FORGIVE, MOVE ON, AND DO WHAT'S RIGHT BY CHIRST.... EACH DAY WE LIVE MAKE IT RIGHT.... MAKE GOD PROUD, MAKE GOD SMILE... DO WHAT YOU KNOW WHAT'S RIGHT TO DO..... THE MAN UP STAIRS IS LISTENING AND HE'S WATCHING YOU.... AND HOW CAN U LIVE BECAUSE IF YOU DON'T FORGIVE... GOD WONT FORGIVE.... LET THE BITTERNESS, THE ANGER, THE HATRED GO... GOD SEES AND GOD KNOW... LOVE YOUR FAMILY IT'S A BEAUTIFUL TOKEN.... FIX IT RIGHT NOW DON'T LEAVE YOUR FAMILY BROKEN!!!!

Call on the Lord

CALL ON THE LORD IN THE TIME OF NEED... THE
LOST OF A LOVE ONE IS SO HARD TO BELIEVE... IT'S
HARD TO DEAL WITH, IT'S HARD TO FACE, IT HURT,
IT'S SAD YOU'RE ANGRY, YOU'RE MAD, CAN'T STOP
CRYING... IT'S NOT FAIR, YOU ASK SOMEONE TO
PLEASE WAKE YOU UP FROM THIS NIGHTMARE....
EACH DAY GO BY, TIME GO ON, IT STILL HURTS... BUT
PRAYER WILL KEEP YOU STRONG!! PRAY...... DON'T
GIVE UP, JUST HOLD ON TIME HEALS ALL WOUNDS.....
BUT IT WILL ALWAYS BE A VOID!!! BUT JUST KEEP THE
FAITH, KEEP PRAYING, AND TRUST IN THE LORD!!!

Know Your Worth

Know your worth, you are never last, you always first... you know what you about, you know what you can do... you know that no one can ever top you.... Keep knowing don't let a man tell you, they may throw punches, and they may throw stones... leave him right where he standing... your life must go on.... No woman deserve to be mistreated, no woman deserve to be used, no woman should never for a man be a fool... but we all make mistakes, you not perfect, he not worth it, you know how much you can take, you may fold, you my bend, and yes you may fall, but stand strong, and stand tall... in the mist of it all... You may can take all you can take, but always know you are built to stand not built to break..... When he gets done thinking you are nothing without him, he's really nothing without you. That's why he holding on so strong, but he's holding on so wrong... because he know once you gone,you are gone...who do he think he is ... talking to you crazy treating you like you are not a queen.. acting ugly and mean, who died and made him king... he better get it together or with him there's no more dating, out there are so many good guys waiting.. he must respect you, he must say he love you, and show you he love you too, he must make your days with him, the most happiest you ever been, he must not only be your man, but also be your friend, around him you should feel safe, to him you should be beautiful, even on your worst day... he should never have anything negative to say! If he loves you he will hold his tongue and walk away! Love is a beautiful thing love doesn't hurt! The only name he should call you is a beautiful queen..... Because you are beautiful, hold down things, love hard, got it going on, the best of the best... he will never find another I don't care how hard he search!!! You are the one and only, honey.... know your worth!!!!

Beautiful Sister Nek

SISTER YOU ARE A BEAUTIFUL PERSON...... INSIDE
AND OUT..... YOU HAVE ME LAUGHING, NO DOUBT.....
COMPARE TO YOU THEY WISH THEY COULD, I
KNOW YOU MORE THEN ANYONE SOMETIMES YOU
MISUNDERSTOOD. YOU ARE A GREAT MOTHER TO
MY NEICE BOTH OF YALL WALK AROUND LOOKING
LIKE A MASTER PIECE! I LOVE YOU! YOU ARE VERY
SPECIAL IN MY LIFE..... WE LAUGH, WE CRY, BUT WE
DON'T ARGUE OR WE DON'T FIGHT. I AM BLESSED TO
HAVE YOU RIGHT HERE WITH ME,WHEN I THINK OF
YOU I SMILE, YOU HAVE CAME A LONG WAY AND OF
YOU I AM VERY PROUD! YOU ARE A STRONG YOUNG
LADY, ONLY IF THEY KNEW, MY GIRL WILL RIDE FOR
ME AND I WILL RIDE FOR YOU! I LOVE WHO YOU
ARE, I LOVE YOUR STYLE, YOU WALK IN THE ROOM
LIKE A STALLION BOLD AND PROUD... WHEN THEY
MADE THAT SONG [I WOKE UP LIKE THIS] THEY

WAS TALKING ABOUT YOU, BECAUSE WAKING UP
LIKE THIS... FOR YOU THIS IS TRUE, KEEP UP THE
GOOD WORK, KEEP DOING WHAT YOU DO, YOU ARE
A BLESSING TO THIS FAMILY AND WE LOVE YOU!!!!

Count Your Blessings

COUNT YOUR BLESSINGS EVERYDAY, IT SHOULD'NT BE HARD, JUST TO SAY THANK U JESUS THANK YOU LORD, FOR THE GOOD TIMES, THE BAD TIMES, THE EASY, THE HARD, COUNT THE LIL BLESSINGS COUNT THE BIG AND THANK THE LORD FOR WHO HE IS, THANK THE LORD FOR YOUR HEALTH AND STRENGTH, THANK THE LORD FOR ALL HE HAS DONE, THANK THE LORD FOR THINGS TO COME, COUNT YOUR BLESSINGS BECAUSE YOU HAVE LIFE, BECAUSE SOME PEOPLE DON'T MAKE IT, AND THE LORD DON'T PUT MORE ON YOU THEN YOU CAN BEAR, THINGS WONT HAPPEN IF YOU CANT TAKE IT. COUNT YOUR BLESSINGS EVERY TIME YOU THINK, BECAUSE GOD BLESS YOU EVERY TIME YOU BLINK, JESUS BLESS YOU EVERYDAY IN EVERYWAY, GOD IS GOOD, GOD IS GREAT, HE'S ALWAYS ON TIME HE'S NEVER LATE. SO STAND STRONG AND KEEP THE FAITH, NO MATTER IF IT'S BRIGHT OR DIM, DON'T FORGET TO THANK

HIM,NO MATTER SUN SHINE OR RAIN DON'T FORGET
TO CALL ON HIS NAME, COUNT YOUR BLESSINGS
AT THE HARDEST POINT OF YOUR LIFE,THANK
THE LORD, KEEP GOING, AND FIGHT, YOU HAVE TO
REALIZE WHAT YOU GO THROUGH IS A JOURNEY TO
GET TO,WHATEVER IT IS THE LORD HAVE DESIGNED
FOR YOU, SO THANK HIM IN ADVANCE BECAUSE
FOR YOU HE HAS PLANS,YOU HAVE INCOME,A ROOF
OVER YOUR HEAD, FAMILY,FRIENDS,FOOD,A CAR,
THANK THE LORD IF YOU HAVE NONE OF THESE
ABOVE, YOU HAVE THE LORD AND HIS LOVE,
AND BECAUSE OF THAT YOU ARE BLESSED. AND
EVERYDAY YOU LIVE, YOU ARE TAUGHT A LESSON,
BUT IN THE MIST OF IT ALL KEEP A THANKFUL
HEART AND ALWAYS COUNT YOUR BLESSINGS!!!!!

Thank You for Loving Me

THANK YOU DAD FOR MAKING OUR LIFE THE BEST THAT WE HAD, IF IT WASN'T FOR DAD, THERE WILL BE NO US. HE BELIEVED IN KEEPING FAMILIES TOGETHER, NOW THAT WAS A MUST, HE WAS THERE THROUGH THICK AND THIN AND ON DAD WE ALL COULD DEPEND... DAD WAS NOT ONLY A GRAND FATHER, HE WAS ALSO A FRIEND, WHO TOLD US HE LOVED US EVERYDAY, AND SHOWED US IN EVERY WAY. WHEN WE NEEDED HIM HE WOULD COME... WOW..... DAD WORK HERE IS DONE, AND I CAN UNDERSTAND WHY HE WAS THE CHOSEN ONE, BECAUSE HE WAS SPECIAL, HE WAS SWEET, AND IT WAS TIME FOR DAD AND JESUS TO MEET! DAD IS IN HEAVEN NOW WHERE HE WILL ALWAYS BE FINE, AND RIGHT ABOUT NOW THIS SHOULD BE A HAPPY TIME... BECAUSE DADS NOT RESTING IN PEACE HE'S LIVING IN PEACE HE'S WITH THE MASTER.... AND THAT'S A RELEIF! SO IF WE WANNA SEE DAD AGAIN

THAT'S WHERE HE WILL BE. DAD IN MY LIFE, YOU
PLAYED A BIG PART, WHEN YOU LEFT YOU TOOK
HALF OF MY HEART, THIS IS THE HARDEST PART TO
LET GO,BECAUSE IF IT WASN'T FOR YOU TELLING
ME ABOUT LIFE, I WILL NEVER KNOW...WHEN YOU
USED TO SAY LIFE IS TOO SHORT..... NOW I SEE... DAD,
I LOVE YOU AND THANK YOU FOR LOVING ME!

Who Am I....?

CAN YOU GUESS WHO I AM? I WILL MAKE YOU KILL, I WILL MAKE YOU STEAL, MISERABLE, I WILL MAKE YOU FEEL... I WILL MAKE YOU WAIST YOUR TIME, I WILL MAKE YOU LOSE EVERYTHING, EVEN YOUR MIND... I WILL MAKE YOU LOSE YOUR MONEY, I WILL MAKE YOU LOSE ALL YOUR THINGS, I WILL MAKE YOU HATE, I WILL MAKE YOU FAKE, BITTERNESS I WILL BRING...I WILL MAKE YOU HAVE UNFORGIVENESS IN YOUR HEART, I WILL MAKE YOU CONFUSED, YOU WONT EVEN KNOW WHERE TO START. I WILL MAKE YOU TURN AGAISNT YOUR FAMILY, I WILL MAKE YOU TURN AGAINST YOUR FRIENDS... I WILL MAKE YOU THINK IT'S COOL BUT YOU WILL BE THE FOOL IN THE END... I WILL MAKE YOU DISOBEY, I WILL MAKE YOU SO BUSY THAT YOU TO BUSY TO PRAY... I WILL MAKE YOU ANGRY, I WILL MAKE YOU MEAN, I WILL MAKE YOU MY PUPPET ON A STRING...YOU WILL BEG, YOU WILL BORROW, ME YOU WILL FOLLOW! I WILL MAKE

YOU LOSE A FIGHT, LOSE YOUR HUSBAND OR WIFE...
KEEP FOLLOWING ME I WILL MAKE YOU LOSE YOUR
LIFE...I WILL MAKE YOU SNAP, KEEP ON COMING
AND FALL RIGHT INTO MY TRAP, I WILL MAKE YOU
FEEL ALONE DOWN AND OUT, I WILL MAKE YOU
NEVER HAVE FAITH AND ALWAYS DOUBT... I AM
YOUR BOSS AND IN THE END I WILL PAY YOU... KEEP
FOLLOWING ME AND YOU WILL BE...STUCK WITH
ME FOR ETERNITY...KEEP COMING, ILL BE WAITING,
TO INTRODUCE MYSELF HI...MY NAME IS SATAN!

In memory of my beautiful mother Carla Neal and

my wonderful grandfather Joe Neal "Dad"

Special Thanks to my lovely daughter Bryana McDowell

About the Author

TRACY NEAL BELIEVE THE LORD IS USING HER TO TOUCH THE LIVES OF OTHERS. SEEING OTHERS HAPPY AND SMILING IS WHAT MAKES HER SMILE. SHE LOVES TO LIFT PEOPLE UP AND GIVE WORDS OF ENCOURAGEMENT, BE A HELPING HAND WHEN NEEDED, A LISTENING EAR WITHOUT JUDGING, TRACY IS A STRONG BEAUTIFUL PERSON INSIDE AND OUT. SHE'S FAMILY ORIENTED HER HAPPIEST MOMENTS ARE SPENDING THEM WITH FAMILY. TRACY IS SUCH A BLESSING

About the Book

THIS BOOK IS VERY INSPIRING AND UPLIFTING,THIS
POETRY BOOK WILL ENCOURAGE YOU, WILL LIFT YOU
UP, AND WILL MAKE YOU THINK ABOUT LIFE, THIS
BOOK IS VERY ANOINTED,AND WILL BE A BLESSING
TO ALL THE READERS IN SOME KIND OF WAY,THIS
IS A MUST HAVE POETRY BOOK IT'S VERY UNIQUE.

Printed in the United States
By Bookmasters